EDITING THE SMALL MAGAZINE

ROWENA FERGUSON

Editing the Small Magazine

SECOND EDITION

REVISED

1 9 7 6

Columbia University Press, New York and London

Library of Congress Cataloging in Publication Data

Ferguson, Rowena.
  Editing the small magazine.

  Bibliography: p. 213
  Includes index.
  1. Journalism.   2. Little magazines.   I. Title.
PN4778.F47   1976   070.4'1   75-12700
ISBN 0-231-03866-6
ISBN 0-231-03970-0 pbk.

❖ ACKNOWLEDGMENTS

My appreciation to many experts and practitioners for help on this second edition: artists, designers, photographers, printers, especially Wayne Hogan and his staff in Nashville.

Rowena Ferguson
Nashville, 1974

CONTENTS

THE MAGAZINE WORLD

The modern magazine arose in the nineteenth century when the development of the technology of printing and the desire of merchants and industrialists for more than local customers intersected. These publications were business enterprises and were always so considered. This does not mean that they did not take an interest in serving their readers, which many of them did in a distinguished way. The readers paid a regular subscription rate but that income was never enough to take care of the payroll and the bills for paper.

In any case the idea was to reach a consumer, not a reader. Consumers were reached through advertising in the pages of the magazines. Fees to advertisers were calculated on the amount of space used and the number of subscribers. Magazines began to fall into several categories: women's, literary, trade magazines, and those for the general reader. Very high circulations were reached, for instance, by *The Woman's Home Companion*, and later *Life*. The arrangement was a good one. Profits rose, and readers, customers, publishers, and advertisers were satisfied. Magazines increased in numbers rapidly. The heyday of this development was the first thirty to forty years of this century.

But at that point television appeared as a competitor for the advertising dollar.

It is easy to see that television, as costly as it is, with its immediacy and its enormous audience, offers irresistible appeal to most kinds of advertisers. One magazine reader said "It was always possible to ignore the printed ads but you can hardly escape the commercials on TV." That, of course, is the idea.

So, under the impact of TV commercials, *The Woman's Home Companion* folded several years ago, in spite of its large circulation, because of commercial difficulties. Gossip in the field said it was deliberately killed through business shenanigans. Then the other big ones began going under: *Redbook, The American Magazine, Collier's,* and that "impregnable" giant in the field, *The Saturday Evening Post.* More recently both *Life* and *Look* have faded.

The anomaly in this abbreviated history is the *Reader's Digest.* For many years the publisher said it survived with no advertising from the quarters that millions of subscribers paid. But the day came when the publisher offered his readers a choice: Expenses had risen to the point where either the subscription price must be raised or ads accepted. Which?, he asked his faithful following. They voted overwhelmingly for ads. Apparently the *Digest* is still going strong, appearing now at grocery counters along with *Family Circle.* A cynical competitor has said that it survives on the formula of "Lincoln's doctor's dog."

It seems to be true that a magazine for "the general reader" is no longer what the public wants, in spite of the *Reader's Digest.* Therefore advertising falls off sharply.

If we can judge by the magazines both old and new with healthy readership, the public is interested in publications addressed to a particular group of readers, with a particular type of content. One on cats, for instance, but not just any cat, a specific breed of cats; and the ads are similarly addressed to customers by manufacturers with a product related to such cats! There is a publication not just on horticulture but on making African violets grow, and on caring for a bonzai. Other hobbies? You name it, and there will be a magazine on it.

Regions and states have started magazines in the tradition of *The New Yorker* and *Arizona Highways.* Most are appropriately not as sophisticated in view and content as the first, nor as handsome in production as the latter. The scholarly journals are still with us, usually under subsidy, but the popularizers, such as *Psychology Today,* are burgeoning. Sociology has spawned several, not all of which have survived, but some are doing well. Even so, it is the approach the public seems to take an interest in now.

The natural sciences are much to the fore. Setting aside that grand old man the *National Geographic* (since it is sponsored by an organization it may receive a subsidy, but it accepts ads), there is a periodical called simply *Minerals.* This magazine is so handsome and alluring that the reader who barely knows what a mineral is can be tempted on receiving a sample copy. The ecology magazines are coming up strong, of course, but unless they have continuing support from a stable and fairly large organization, they will go under because of the cost of printing almost anything. Ecology is too generalized a subject to attract ads. And if they settle for mimeographing or some cheap form of printing, second-class postage will be hard to face. As expected, magazines in the computer field usually subsidized by a professional group have come along in the last three years. The list goes on and on but we can already note many differences between magazines such as these and *The Saturday Evening Post* in its original incarnation.

❊ CHARACTERISTICS OF THE SMALL MAGAZINE

Last year 1400 new magazines were registered in the U.S. This means that magazines are not gone, they have merely changed their character. A large proportion of them were of the kind just described. And a large proportion of that kind are what this book means by "the small magazine." Now is the time to sort out the characteristics of the small magazine and its place in the magazine world.

The word "small," as used in this title, does not refer to physical size, or circulation, or budget. It is used to distinguish it from the commercial or "consumer" magazine. The small magazine may be large in format, it may have a sizable circulation, it may be limited to a four-page fold (e.g., the newsletter of a small organization) or it may go to 96 pages (e.g., the house organ of a large national business). Or it may be small in the usual sense of a very limited operation. Small magazines are different from one another in a wide variety of ways. The thousands of small magazines that constitute the majority of those published today have a large place in the magazine world and employ a commensurate number of people as "editors" and other workers.

One of the things, however, that most of them have in common is that they are sponsored by some sort of group or organization. These can range from the Audobon club to a local association for retarded children with 500 members.

In spite of all this variety, however, we can identify fundamental and important characteristics in which these magazines are more or less alike and by which they are distinguished from commercial magazines.

In the first place, because the small magazine is the child of a parent body, it exists to serve the special purposes of that body. For this reason the magazine may be said to be the voice of its sponsor, with a message, a point of view, or a program to promote among its readers.

Second, this parent body, while it is the publisher of a magazine, is not of itself in the publishing business; in fact it may be quite remote from the influences of the magazine world as seen from the standpoint of the commercial magazine.

Third, the small magazine carries little or no advertising, and in any case it is not supported by advertisements which may appear in it.

Fourth, financial support in most cases comes from a subsidy obtained either by membership dues or through a budget appropriation. Therefore, the magazine is not expected to make money, frequently not even to pay its own bills, although some nonconsumer publications are self-supporting. In other words, it is not primarily a business venture.

Fifth, circulation is limited and often controlled. Many nonconsumer magazines are given away, especially those distributed to the customers or employees of a company or an industry.

It should be recognized here that the memberships of a few organizations are so extensive that their magazines constitute legitimate advertising media. They solicit ads and for the most part assume the character of the commercial magazine. Some large industrial concerns use so many magazines in their employee and public relations programs that they can almost be said to be in the publishing business. Frequently these concerns hire outside agencies to produce all their publications.

Typical small magazines are faced with several common problems that arise out of their specialized character.

First, having a parent body, the publication is not always obliged to make its way under its own steam. The members or persons associated with the sponsoring group will be predisposed in its favor. Thus, the magazine has a number of ready-made advocates and profits by whatever prestige or good will the organization carries among its constituents. In short, the parent body materially assists the magazine in getting a favorable response from its readers.

There is, however, the reverse side of this coin. The magazine is responsible to its parent body and is not free, being limited by a policy and practice specified by that body. The editorial policy must be consistent with the point of view and the program of the sponsoring organization. The editor of a nonconsumer magazine is likely to be at least loosely tied to a party line. This relation to the parent body also means that the content of the magazine is much more restricted than is that of a publication circulating to the general public. Much of the content stems from the organization's special field of interest and, furthermore, is tailored to the organization's particular purposes. It is necessary, therefore, to provide for hand tooling much of the content on the basis of an inside view of the sponsoring body. It is equally necessary to take care that this inside view does not result in an overly narrow outlook.

Second, the small magazine has a more or less captive audience. This fact poses both an advantage and a disadvantage. It is an advantage in that the editor knows exactly who his readers are and can usually arrive at a fairly accurate mental picture of their habits, interests, and impulses without the elaborate market research which commercial magazines sometimes employ. In case the parent body is a membership organization, he can arrange a considerable amount of first-hand contact with his readers. Another value of having captive readers is that the publication is not subjected to the rigors of building and maintaining circulation. But again there is a reverse side. The disadvantage is that the readers may be taken for granted too easily. Because the readers are going to "get" the magazine anyway, that is, because it is going to be handed to them free, since they work for a company or they belong to an organization, the editor and others responsible for the publication may tend to lose sight of reader interest. When the editor forgets the reader the magazine becomes what the editor or the head office wants, or thinks the reader should have, rather than what the reader wants. Although the periodical still circulates, the reader feels no stake in it and may even drop an issue in the waste-basket unopened. Particular vigilance is necessary to compensate for the lack of the spur provided by open-market circulation.

Third, the small magazine is often supervised and even edited by persons who are professionals in the field of the magazine's specialty but inexperienced as editors, with the result that the editorial work may be strictly amateur in quality. As a consequence the publication loses reader appeal and suffers from poor communication. The concern should, of course, be to maintain the professional standing of the content and at the same time to achieve recognized editorial standards.

Thus it can be seen that the nonconsumer magazine occupies its own niche in the magazine world, with its peculiar problems, concerns, and opportunities. It shares many technical editorial concerns with all other magazines, but it requires very special consideration with regard to editorial policy and planning.

❖ THE EDITOR AND HIS JOB

Now that we have taken a glimpse at the history of the magazine as a form of publishing, have found the place of the small magazine in this world, and have considered its specialized characteristics, we should certainly have a word to say about the editor. He (or she) is really the maker and shaker of the whole business, even if there is a competent staff to take care of some important chores.

The editor is at the center of a complicated web of operations, and supervises the entire process from contemplating the first blank sheet of paper to getting the completed magazines into the hands of the readers. This does not mean that he is a czar making all the decisions. He maintains many relationships of a helpful character and he learns to minimize the less helpful ones. The role of his colleagues has already been hinted at but will be given more emphasis in later chapters.

Aside from these relationships, which vary with each type of magazine, he is continually involved in the editorial process, perhaps carrying forward two or more steps in that process at one time. Look at the table of contents of this book. The chapter titles indicate in a reasonably chronological order the several steps in the process and chapter content describes how the editor may carry them out effectively.

We should really ask at this point what kind of person the editor should be and what qualifications and competencies he or she should exhibit. Here is a list that may be suggestive:

1. *Understanding of his readers.* This is the first and prime qualification of the good editor, for which there is no substitute. He must know who his readers are, how they think, what they want, what they worry about, how they live, and how they are related to the magazine. To be familiar with his readers is the first step in communicating with them, and that is the function of the editor of any magazine. This qualification is especially important for the editor of the small magazine, which is often the organ of a specialized group. In many cases the editor is a member of that group. It is not enough, however, for the editor to represent his readers directly. He must also be able to stand apart from them so as to

interpret and analyze their responses with some degree of objectivity. For this reason, the editor need not necessarily be drawn from the magazine's constituency, because with imagination he can often put himself in his readers' shoes. The thing he must necessarily do is respect his readers, neither standing in awe of them nor talking down to them.

2. *Good editorial judgment.* Reduced to its simplest terms, the editor's job is making one decision after another at several levels of significance. "Shall the magazine be pocket-size and therefore easily handled, or tabloid-size and allow for smashing layouts?" "Is color worth the extra cost?" "Does this manuscript have general reader appeal or does it just suit my personal taste?" "Can I cut a thousand words out of this story and have anything left?" "Shall I replace the editorial page with a letters-to-the-editor department?" These are the kinds of decisions that face an editor every day. As has been indicated also, the process flows according to a more or less strict timetable, so that nearly always a moment arrives when further reflection on a question is impossible and the editor must make up his mind.

Accordingly, a qualification of the good editor is that he must know how to make decisions, and be willing and able to assume responsibility for them. If he lacks these qualities, his pages will reflect indecision, vagueness, and ambiguity, and the magazine as a whole will be weak and without character.

Sound editorial judgment requires imagination, a quality the editor shares with other craftsmen. This quality of mind and spirit enables an editor to reach beyond conventional formulas, to shake loose the cut-and-dried method, to discover values that lie below the surface. And preeminently, it allows him to think like his readers.

3. *Capacity for visualization.* Even a cursory look reveals that the editorial process deals with visual materials and concepts. A good editor is able to predict to some degree how things are going to look in his pages. He can visualize a specific issue so as to know that three consecutive pages with no pictures will produce a long dry spell for the reader's eye. He sees in his mind two titles on facing pages placed next to each other and knows they will cancel each other in getting the reader's attention. He knows in advance that pictures of various shapes on one page confuse and discourage the reader. His eye tells him that cropping off the top and right-hand side of a photograph will perhaps sharpen its point and give it more dramatic impact. In a group of twelve photographs for an article, he can select the best three or five for his particular purpose. He looks at several type faces and decides that one will have a bright sparkling effect while another will give an impression of "color" and solidity. In all these ways, and many more, he uses his capacity for visualization.

4. *Ability to work on a time schedule.* This point bears repeating, even if it has been hinted at already, because nothing will foul the editorial routine as much as missed deadlines. An editor should therefore be the kind of person for whom a time schedule is something less than a work of the devil. Some people find it impossible to adjust themselves to the calendar and to the necessity of doing a job at a specific time. Such persons make unhappy and ineffective editors.

Some other people are able to keep a blueprint of the editorial process in their mind's eye and to time their work to its requirements. The comforting word should be said that practice improves this ability to the point where the experienced editor is able to function within his timetable without undue wear and tear. That is not to say he achieves this fortunate state without pressure. In an editorial office, no matter how expertly managed, some jobs sometimes must be carried on under forced draft.

In addition to the general qualifications listed above, some specific skills are required of an editor. Four can be identified as follows:

1. *Capacity for communication.* To be able to communicate with people means to know what catches attention and elicits a response. A magazine may contain good writing, clever illustrations, and sound editorials, but unless the reader feels it speaks to him, it will not survive. In order to make his pages speak convincingly, the editor uses the principles of communication as well as he can, in as many ways as possible. It is particularly important that he do so in a specialized magazine because, more frequently than not, it has a program of some sort to sell or interpret to its readers— perhaps a new policy of an industrial concern or a service project of a club. He will therefore make sure not only that his content is accurate and interesting, but also that it is likely to impress the reader as significant in general and relevant in particular to him. The magazine must talk *to* people, not *at* them.

In achieving this impression on the reader, the manuscript

by the way it is written plays a large part. A useful maxim is that any manuscript must be not just good, but good for something—that is, it must be meaningful to the individuals who make up the magazine's constituency. It must tell them something that they want to know, or that will instruct, entertain, edify, or inspire them. Of course, readers may not have been aware ahead of time that they would be so affected. To this end, writers employ such techniques of communication as concreteness in presenting information, a personalized approach, and a graphic style. Editors look for this type of writing, and often they encourage or train their contributors in ways of being more communicative. This is particularly important in the case of those magazines which by their very nature must frequently use material prepared by amateurs, people for whom writing for publication is not a primary skill—possibly a nurse or a plant superintendent or a stenographer who has been designated to collect news items from her department for a house organ.

Further, in order to maintain communication with readers, every magazine has a particular slant to which its contents are tailored. The slant is directly related to and determined by the magazine's purpose, character, and policy, that is, its over-all profile. Therefore an editor may say to a writer that his piece is well written but not "slanted for our book." (Most printers and some editors refer to any job as a "book.")

To illustrate this point in another way, let us say the magazine for a national woman's service club is considering an article on the program of a welfare institution in which the club has an interest. The article's point of view, language, and emphasis would be quite different from what they would be in an article on the same subject circulated among sociologists.

All the other elements in the book—pictures, titles, blurbs, as well as the way they are put together, that is, the layout—play their part in this process of communication.

2. *Skill in language.* Inasmuch as an editor works primarily as a wordsmith, he should feel at home with words and should be able to handle the mechanics of the English language easily and competently. He should understand the basic structure of the sentence, so that when necessary he can skillfully rebuild with his blue pencil the awkward and clouded sentences that crop up in even the most acceptable manuscript. Then if he knows the nature and function of the paragraph, he has a grasp of the technique of organizing material for readability. Often a second- or third-rate article can be turned into a first-rate one by organizing the content so as to achieve form and movement.

3. *Understanding of the principles of design.* The packaging of the book—its size, its cover, and the appearance of its page—is extremely important. Unattractive design can render perfectly good text ineffective. An editor, therefore, should have an eye for form and the ability to compose and arrange shapes in ways that are pleasing and satisfying. A sense of proportion, of balance, and also of imbalance or disequilibrium, and an understanding of the way the eye moves across a double-page spread are all needed to produce layouts that enhance the text and make the pages speak.

It is necessary for many editors of nonconsumer magazines to make their own layouts, although some will have the services of an art editor. This does not mean that every editor must also be an artist in the sense of being able to draw and paint. It does mean that he must think graphically, always conscious of how the pictures, the heads, the type masses, and the white spaces on each of his pages go together. Do they produce a congenial composition, or do they fall apart in nervous disorder? Much can be learned through practice with pencils, rulers, and other simple tools.

4. *Understanding of the production process.* The production process refers to the steps by which the raw material of a magazine—the separate manuscripts and illustrations—are turned into bound books ready for distribution. A knowledge of production processes involves an understanding of the ways in which type is set, cuts are made, printing is done, and printed sheets are folded and bound.

To become familiar with these matters, the editor works closely with and is guided by his printer. But the surer his understanding, the better he can exploit the advantages of the printing process used and minimize its limitations. Furthermore, the greater the understanding of the process, the greater the chance for avoiding unnecessary expenditure of money and time.

A good editor knows the kind of machines that are used in producing his magazine and the way they are operated. Even with only a rudimentary knowledge of the printing process, he will know what happens to his copy from the time the printer receives it until the finished issues are delivered. All this information helps him in answering such questions as: Can I increase the size of the book? What screen shall I use for the half-tones? Can I put any text or pictures in the margins of the pages? On which pages can I use color? How may I cut the cost of alterations in the proofs?

Now that we have an overview of the editorial process and the editor's task and prerequisites, we can launch immediately into a discussion of how the various parts of that process are effectively carried on.

The purpose of this book is to provide a practical guide for persons who are responsible for the issuance of this type of magazine. We believe that among these persons might be students of journalism, beginners working out their editorial apprenticeships, editors of amateur status, professional editors who are inexperienced in the small magazine field, executives responsible for such magazines. The chapters deal with accepted methods and techniques used in getting out such periodicals, with standards and sources of content material, with various matters relating to physical appearance, and with executive and administrative questions. This content is described in concrete terms, with specific illustrations of points made and principles delineated. We hope in this way to stimulate the thought, imagination, and energy of the editor so as to increase his effectiveness and to enhance his feelings of success and satisfaction.

CHAPTER ONE

EDITORIAL PLANNING

With this chapter we begin detailed discussion of the steps in the editorial process. They are described, one by one in the succeeding chapters, as nearly as possible in chronological order, that is, in the order in which they would be carried out in the editorial office. The editor goes through these steps, performing the jobs required approximately in this order on any one issue. But, because he rarely is dealing with just one issue at any given time, actually he carries through two or more steps at once. This is one reason that the editorial job is complicated.

The first step is editorial planning, which has as its goal the assurance that the pages of the magazine are filled with the appropriate kind of content. This planning is quite long-range and takes into consideration not one but several future issues. It takes place long before press time, and is one of the ways in which many important editorial decisions are reached. The effective magazine is in large part the result of good editorial planning. In this chapter we start with the specific functions of planning and then describe how to organize and carry out regularly scheduled planning conferences.

❖ VALUES OF PLANNING

1. Planning makes it possible to maintain a consistent slant or personality of a magazine.

Every successful magazine is built to a formula, that is, it exhibits a definite personality or profile. Making up your contents from whatever pieces happen to be handy or easiest to arrange will definitely blur the book's personality.

For example, suppose that the national convention of your organization has just been held, or that the board of directors of your company at its quarterly meeting has announced a new employee policy. You are close to the deadline of the issue in which such an event should be reported. If you have not made advance plans, you will be severely curtailed in what you can do. You will have no pictures, certainly none made especially for your book (which would be best), and it may be too late to get them from another source, such as a newspaper in the city in which the event took place. (An organization's meetings are often not held in the city where the office of its magazine is located.) You may not be able at this time to get an eyewitness, firsthand story. If this is true, your story will be at best a pale recollection by someone who was there but who was not thinking of the experience in terms of its significance for the magazine. It will probably not be possible to get quotes from people directly involved, for example, the new officers elected for the national organization, or an interpretation of the new policy from the chairman of the board. Contributions like these can be solicited by mail, but that is a time-consuming and unreliable way of getting copy. So about all you can do is talk to someone who was on the spot and possibly to the people involved (new officers and chairman). Perhaps long-distance telephone calls may be necessary. You may thus put a warmed-over story through your typewriter. Unless you are exceptionally clever, your readers will recognize that your story is secondhand. If the purpose of your book is to reflect your institution, you have seriously distorted that reflection by poor editorial handling of a significant event in the institution's program.

On the other hand, had you planned well you would have decided far ahead of the meeting how and by whom it would be reported in the magazine. You, or someone selected and instructed by you, would have been on hand to know in detail what took place, to talk to key people, to take or arrange for appropriate pictures, and to write a firsthand, lively story from an angle suited to your purposes. You would have enough material of the right kind to produce a magazine feature commensurate in significance with the event itself, an item capable of communicating that significance to your readers.

2. Planning makes possible an over-all and long-range strategy for getting across a magazine's message.

At regular intervals, the editor and other responsible persons should review the purposes of the magazine and decide on its specific functions for six weeks or six months, a year, or two years in the future, depending upon your type of magazine. Definite features for the magazine should then be planned in the light of these decisions.

3. Planning guards against a procedure that is too oppor-
tunistic. The catch-as-catch-can editorial policy is a special
temptation to the editor of a relatively small operation. Let us
say he issues a local bulletin published as a four-page fold.
Such a publication does not require anyone's full time, and
for that reason it is often not given enough time, especially
not enough time at the right time. So here, for example, is
an editor who finds he has to send something to the printer
tomorrow! He combs through his files to see what he's got to
fill up the pages. An editor of any kind of magazine finding
himself in such a situation very often is courting disaster.
The least of an editor's worries should be filling his pages. He
should be worrying about how he can possibly stretch his
book to get in all of the fine expertly planned features.

This harried man who must get out his bulletin should
have taken a couple of days long ago to start in motion some
basic plans for at least three issues in advance, making a
schedule of content for each one, writing letters, putting
through telephone calls, sending memos, all of which were
intended to produce copy of one kind or another. Between
this time of preliminary planning and press day, he would
probably have had to check on others as well as himself and
perhaps make some changes in his plans. But when the
twenty-fourth hour arrives, he would know what he has to fill
his pages and is satisfied that although all of it may not be as
good as he would like, none of it is a makeshift and a last
resort.

It is important to realize that getting to press satisfactorily
depends as much on what you have done six months previously as upon what you do on the day of the printer's

deadline. Most of the advance work comes under the head of editorial planning.

4. Planning enables an editor to handle inevitable emergencies without loss of significant values.

No matter how forehanded you are, you are sure to face a day when nothing works out as expected. The photographer on whom you have been depending has come down with a virus; an important manuscript has turned out all wrong; you have had to pinch-hit for someone else in the office and your editorial is not written. In this situation you dig into your inventory of manuscripts and pictures—features of various kinds that will be good in any issue of your magazine. They are not earmarked for specific issues, or, if they are, they will fit just as well in earlier ones. At any one time an editor should have on hand in his files more material than he has an immediate use for. This material constitutes his manuscript and illustration inventory, and he should make sure that this inventory does not fall below a certain point. When he begins scraping the bottom of the barrel, he is headed for trouble.

Editorial planning, then, includes the development of many features which are not scheduled and which serve as a cushion against emergencies. In some editorial offices this development proceeds as far as making layouts, so that, for example, a double-page feature, ready to send to press, could be substituted in very short order for a scheduled one that failed to materialize. Good planning then involves keeping the inventory at its proper level.

5. Planning encourages better work on the part of contributors.

This is true because it gives writers, or artists and photographers, sufficient time to do their best work. It also means that the editor has a chance to interpret to them more fully what he wants, to give them whatever guidance they need, and even to allow for the correction of mistakes. Moreover, advance planning has a psychological advantage. An artist or an author is likely to impart more significance to a feature he sees carefully planned than to one that is being rushed through on the spur of the moment.

Looking ahead and working up specific features in advance has the further advantage of allowing the editor some second thoughts. It is good to mull over an idea while deciding how to treat it most appropriately. Perhaps the first way, on further reflection, has turned out to be overly elaborate and impractical or not worth the editorial time involved; perhaps it is better to arrange an interview with a person than to ask him to write an article; perhaps there is another and better source of photographs for a projected feature; possibly this idea would fit into the schedule more suitably another week or month or even next year. However, this does not mean putting off decisions indefinitely or even delaying decisions beyond the point when new light on them may be expected.

In this respect, magazine editing differs markedly from newspaper editing. Newspapers by their very nature must be edited at high speed, and many editorial decisions must be made between one moment and the next. But the small magazine is not on a news schedule. Also, it has a longer life expectancy than the daily paper, which is outdated, or at least superseded, in twenty-four hours. The magazine editor can afford somewhat more leisurely planning, and his book deserves it.

6. Planning allows for flexibility, for taking advantage of emergent situations; it should encourage flexibility.

With all due regard for the values of editorial planning, it is quite possible for the plans to be too fixed and final. The editor should always be so attuned to what is happening in his readers' world that he recognizes a break when he sees one. Such a break may be an unexpected event or a developing situation that is a hot spot of interest for his readers. This is the now-or-never story. Faced with the possibility of such a story, the editor tears up his carefully made advance plans (or saves them for a duller day if possible) and goes into speedy action on this new line of interest. He must not yield to the temptation to let a good story slip by because he has had his book already made up. He must not let himself be a slave to his own plans. Nor should he plan so far ahead that he loses any sense of the contemporary. In fact, the alert editor lives in both the present and the future. He is continually shifting back and forth in time.

A magazine turns out better, however, when well-laid plans are changed to take care of the unexpected than when there is little planning and everything becomes the unexpected. Good planning is flexible, not haphazard; it frees the editor to take advantage of a sudden opportunity.

Let us now turn to a consideration of the techniques and practices of planning.

❖ SCHEDULE

In a schedule of operations for the editorial process, regular sessions for planning should be indicated. The number of these occasions depends upon the frequency of issue and the nature of the book. The more often the book appears and the more complex its contents, the more frequent and elaborate must be the planning sessions. For a weekly or biweekly magazine of four, eight, sixteen, or more pages, one session every two months for long-range planning seems appropriate. For a monthly of the same number of pages, a session once every three months is adequate. And for a quarterly, two sessions per year seems sufficient.

These long-range planning sessions should be scheduled not less than six weeks to two months ahead of the first deadline in the editorial process. In other words, the editor should allow himself at least that much time to carry out any plans made at the conference before he must have copy and illustrations in hand.

For a weekly, everything moves at a more rapid rate, although there may be compensation in the fact that the book will probably have fewer pages and less complicated material. In any case, long-range planning for a weekly should take place at least three weeks in advance of the first deadline and ten weeks ahead of publication date.

Planning for a quarterly requires a much simpler schedule, two issues being considered at each semiannual session. The timing would approximate that of a monthly.

Dates for planning should be set in the schedule as firmly

as any other deadline and should not be bypassed or post-
poned except in extraordinary circumstances. In most cases
more people than the editor will be involved, which means
that the editor should find dates sufficiently in advance to
meet the convenience of all persons concerned. Then he will
see that they are notified at the time the dates are agreed
upon and reminded shortly before each one. It is in his interest to have good attendance at the conferences, so he leaves
no stone of encouragement unturned.

❖ PEOPLE INVOLVED IN PLANNING

The personnel of the planning group should certainly include the editor's executive, that is, the person to whom he is
administratively responsible, and any other persons on the
staff of the organization who have a stake in the magazine.
Certain people responsible for program, to whom reference is
made below, are in this category. Any persons who have substantial and regular writing assignments, either on or outside
the staff, will make good contributions to planning and will
benefit from the experience. Sometimes these people are
known as contributing editors. Sometimes, especially in the
case of an employee publication, they represent branches or
units of the business or industry and serve as reporters. Such
people are valuable in the planning conference because they
are close to the constituency. They in turn may learn how to
be more skillful in carrying out their assignments.

It may be necessary to make appropriate arrangements for
these people to be released from their regular duties to attend

planning conferences. This is an additional reason for scheduling them well in advance, keeping their frequency to a minimum, and making adequate preparations.

If the editor has one or more assistants with editorial, not clerical or secretarial, responsibilities, they should be a part of the planning group. They can do their work more intelligently when they are in on the process from the beginning, and the editor is relieved of extensive interpretation.

In most cases direct representation from the readers at conferences does not work well. The planning group should strive for an editorial or a semieditorial point of view; that is, it should think about the readers with whatever objectivity can be achieved. The subjective responses of your readers are valuable to you in so far as they can tell you "what I like" or "what I want." Therefore, although their reactions are essential in the planning process, when personally made they are a drawback. Too quickly laymen stop reacting like readers, and start thinking like editors.

It may be a good idea to organize a group of readers related to the magazine, but not for the purpose of planning.

❖ PREPARATIONS FOR PLANNING

In preparing for planning sessions, the editor makes a survey of past issues or brings up to date surveys made for earlier conferences. He looks critically at the issues published since the last time the planning group met and examines the way they fit into the over-all program of the past year. First, he makes an analysis of content in which he classifies features according to topic and also according to type. For example, topical classifications might be features on people in the organization, events, travel and vacation, history, places, issues, work of local units, interpretation of public affairs, guidance to members. The specific topics are determined by the nature and function of the magazine. Under each topical classification, specific subject matter may also be listed. Types of features may be editorials, correspondence with readers, news from local units, illustrated articles, picture stories, departments, and the like.

A summary of these classifications will produce a picture of the magazine over the last year. It may reveal gaps and imbalance in content; it will indicate whether certain features are requiring an inordinate amount of space; it will show up any trend toward tangential content. This picture should coincide with the personality of the magazine. If it does not, it says plainly that the book is not on its slant. (Printers and sometimes editors refer to any job as a "book.") When that happens, the editor and any others responsible should decide whether the planning has been poor, or whether the slant should be changed.

A planning group should use a survey of past issues also to judge how efficient the planning has been. If the features proposed have not turned out well on the pages of the magazine, perhaps they were not soundly conceived. A critical analysis of this kind will sharpen the judgment and refine the ideas of the group's members.

As a further preparation for a planning session, the editor should collect and organize accounts of reader reaction he has received since he last reported. They may come through personal contact or by correspondence in one way or another. Reaction may or may not be reflected in circulation. If the readers are the same as the membership of the organization, the trend may be observed. If the readership is captive, as it is with company magazines, circulation will not reflect reader reaction, and the editor must use other means to get it. Whatever the situation, it is well for each planning conference to work against a background of recent reader response.

It is quite appropriate also for the editor to describe any problems he is facing, not problems of personnel or intramural relationships, but problems in getting out the magazine. They may concern his schedule, or the production process, or his own responsibilities. Perhaps he has trouble getting first-rate reporting of events or program. If he must depend on persuading any likely person who happens to be on hand to send in a story, he cannot expect very good copy. Some different arrangement should be made. Perhaps his difficulty is in obtaining suitable pictures, or perhaps he thinks the book needs more, or fewer, staff-written features. These are appropriate items for the agenda of a planning conference.

On a magazine of any size, that is, one requiring at least one full-time person, the planning sessions will be formal enough to require an agenda—a list of things to discuss and decide. It is the duty of the editor to prepare the agenda in advance and submit it as a basis for the work of the conference. Other members of the group should be asked to submit items for the agenda, either in advance of the meeting or as soon as it convenes. Having an agenda serves the double purpose of enlisting the interest of the people in a significant task (everyone hates meetings where nothing is done) and of keeping them to the job at hand in case there is a tendency to fritter away time in casual conversation. Preparing the agenda also helps the editor organize his ideas about his needs and his work.

❀ *IDEAS FOR CONTENT*

By far, the biggest part of editorial planning is dreaming up ideas for content. Strangely enough, this is the place where most inexperienced or amateur editors find the going toughest. So let's consider in detail where these ideas come from.

THE NEEDS OF YOUR READERS. In the previous chapter, the list of qualifications of an editor was headed by knowledge about and an understanding of his readers. It is in devising the content of his book that an editor makes largest use of this understanding. When he plans features, he is really thinking of his readers; he is not thinking in a vacuum or making up ideas out of the blue. He makes them up out of what he knows about his readers at first hand, added to what his creative imagination tells him about them.

First of all, what are your readers interested in? Being people, they share certain interests with all other people. Chief among these is an interest in themselves and other people like themselves. Accordingly they are concerned about the problems they face and the needs they feel. (We are using problems here to mean not only things that are troublesome but also situations that must be handled.) Identifying some of these problems, big and little, and some of these needs of your constituency provides grist for features.

Let us say you are planning an employee publication. A common event among workers is the arrival of a new person in a department—common in the sense of ordinary and also in the sense that every worker has shared in this experience repeatedly. You therefore decide on a treatment of this problem. You know that new employees receive some orientation from the personnel people in your organization, so that is not your angle. It should not be, in any case, for an employee publication should try not to be the voice of the company administration. It seems a realistic approach to let the people directly concerned speak about it. So you think of a double article—one from the point of view of the old-timer on what is expected of the new recruit, words of wisdom to a novice, etc., and the other from the point of view of the new arrival on how he feels about his new job, what he expects from the old-timers, etc. Two people could be chosen to write these companion pieces, but unless they really know how to write and are willing to speak up, the result may be disappointing. A better method is for you to interview several people in each category and devise a composite reaction. You would use names or not, according to the sensibilities of the people. It goes without saying that you would not include anything to cause embarrassment or discomfort to anyone. Even so, you could get enough content for quite meaty articles, which might be most readable if worked up in a light style.

Another common interest among employees is working conditions. Here is a rich mine of content for your book. Take air conditioning, for instance. People argue about it vociferously, and yet few really know anything about it, although they may be subjected to many kinds during an urban summer. It is a safe guess that if your building is air conditioned, reactions to it are loud and intense—for, against, and neutral. So why not in consultation with your engineers, and maybe reading up on the subject, develop a piece on thermal dynamics which would explain exactly what is expected of your type of air-conditioning system, what happens and why; how those who like it can get the most out of it and how those who do not can modify its effect?

Suppose now you are the editor of a magazine circulated to professional women, the journal of a service club, for example. You will think long and hard on the specific problems and interests of this group. What about an article exploring the kinds of insurance coverage that are most advantageous for people like your readers? This would probably have to be done by an expert rather than your staff, although the expert might need staff guidance in communicating the technical aspects of the subject.

Or suppose you are editing the magazine of an industrial association. If your readers are people inside the industry, you will plan features on the technology of the industry, and on its competition; you will think of stories about specific companies, possibly one that has made a good comeback, or about an individual responsible for an innovation or advance in the field. If your readers are customers or the general public, you will think of ways they are related to your product. Most of the current magazines for the customers of the automobile industry concentrate their content on interesting places, on the sound theory that the readers use their cars for travel. But it would be just as sound to assume a broader scope for content. Good advice on how to buy an automobile—all are ideas for content in which most any car owner would be interested.

Magazines of ideas, including scholarly journals and journals of opinion or affairs, although more intellectualized in content than some other types of periodicals, should be just as firmly rooted in the interests and problems of their readers. They should studiously avoid articles on esoteric subjects in which no one is interested, no matter how good they might be, as well as the thesis abstracts with conclusions that will not matter to anyone. Research required for an academic degree is not necessarily good for magazine treatment. Editors who plan these journals should ask themselves: What questions are our readers asking? What are they thinking about? And then they should plan features which will contribute some answers and encourage further thinking. It is also a good idea to ask: what *should* our readers be thinking about and why? One of the functions of the journal of ideas is to alert its readers to developing thought in its field, to apprise them of trends and events, to interpret activity in their area of concern. When a feature is planned along these lines, care should be taken to explain why its subject is significant and why it deserves attention. In other words, the relevance of the feature to the experience of the reader should be pointed out explicitly. These are equally sound techniques for other types of magazines as well.

As one last example of planning according to the concerns of readers, take the case of an editor of a magazine for older adults. Several small magazines for this group are now being marketed. The specialized problems and unique situations of this section of the population furnish plenty of ideas for content. Articles on the normal process of aging and how to cope with it would be popular, as well as angles on personal problems, such as how to live with your daughter-in-law, or how to manage when living alone. Features about places are especially appropriate for the reader whose travel is confined to the armchair variety. And naturally the experience, not to say "trauma," of retirement is a suitable field for features.

The more persistent and concrete your thinking on the needs and interests of your readers, the more your ideas will flow freely and eloquently. Probably you have already surmised that the editorial planning conference gives much impetus to originality and creativity. Yet no matter how fertile the imagination of an editor is; he cannot supply all the ideas for content and should not be expected to do so. Other persons in contact with the magazine's readership should be able to make valuable suggestions, especially through the planning conference. Of course, suggestions could be received informally at any time. It may be that a passing suggestion, while containing the germ of a good idea, will not be formulated in terms of a magazine piece. This is one function of the editor—to translate any workable suggestion of this sort into a publishable feature. The editor will naturally be able to think more journalistically than other people who do not have his special skills. In fact, that is a reason for employing a practicing journalist on a nonconsumer magazine, rather than relying entirely upon the services of someone without this experience, no matter how competent the latter may be in the magazine's field.

THE PURPOSE OF THE MAGAZINE. Here is another key to the content of your book. An editor should frequently ask himself: What is this book supposed to do? And he should follow that question with: Is the content fulfilling the purpose? What kinds of content will fulfill that purpose?

Employee publications are so various that they serve many different purposes. But no one publication should be expected to do too many things; it should concentrate on one purpose, or at most on a few closely related purposes. For instance, the purpose may be to serve as the voice of the employees themselves—to be their group expression. Such a periodical is not so much *for* the readers as *of* the readers, a distinction that should be clearly reflected in its content. For a magazine of this kind, many features will be planned about the readers, both individually and collectively. If the readership is large enough, it will go in heavily for personal news. But with a small number of readers, everybody would already have such news by word of mouth before it could get into print. In fact, a magazine for an organization, business, or industry with only a few employees, who can be expected to know one another on a face-to-face basis, does not need to feature this kind of news. Stories about their group activities, both on and off the job, would better serve its purpose. A good use of pictures would be appropriate, for people are always interested in photographs of themselves and people they know, even when the shots are not particularly significant. A roving candid camera report in each issue would pull reader attention. Of course, each report should be angled to tell a story.

Let us say, on the other hand, that the purpose of an employee periodical is to serve more precisely as a house organ, that is, to interpret the organization, business, or industry to

the employees, to foster their sense of belonging, and to encourage their feeling of personal, intelligent, and significant
participation. Then features on the work or program of the
firm are appropriate, especially those with a wide focus. Most
employees are not in a position to see much beyond their
own more or less minute operations, and often they do not
understand how their particular jobs fit into the total work of
the organization. For example, a feature on the advertising
program of a national industry explaining why and how it is
planned and promoted should interest the people who produce the merchandise. Reports of special achievements of
employees, individually or collectively; stories of pertinent
activities of a union and of an employers' association; interpretation of events that will influence the work program of
the organization; news of important changes in personnel—
these are all "naturals" for the content of this book.

THE MESSAGE OF THE MAGAZINE. This factor in planning
content is closely related to purpose, but it is important in itself, especially for a magazine that serves an organization
with member units. The message will reflect the group's purpose and will likely attempt to sell the readers on the significance and importance of the organization; in other words, it
will try to keep the membership interested, active, and grow-
ing. If there is a large number of local units, members may
support and receive both a national and a local journal.

This is the kind of magazine that can be so easily taken for
granted by its constituency that they never read it. Usually it
comes automatically with the payment of dues, and therefore
the editor cannot assume initial motivation on the part of the
reader. With this handicap at the very beginning, the book

must literally capture the attention of the reader and then build and sustain his interest. Accordingly, the content must not only set forth and interpret the message, but it must do so in terms that communicate quickly to the reader.

Success stories are always good. Such stories can be developed from reports of well-planned and well-executed projects, either at the national or regional level. Features that demonstrate the purpose of the organization have selling value because they indicate to the reader how the program relates to him. For example, the journal of a professional association might very well plan various items of content that give counsel on how to maintain professional standards and, as a corollary, on professional fees or salaries commensurate with the standards. Of course, improved professional techniques represent a suitable area of content and help the reader directly.

For a magazine serving a federation of clubs, leagues, guilds, and the like, ideas for local programs and interesting group activities offer a wide field for possible features. They should be developed in such a way that the reader is impressed with their significance and feasibility. People generally react favorably to suggestions of things to do in a field in which they already have an interest. Also such material stimulates local program planners and in turn enhances the appeal of the local unit among its members. The editor may provide this kind of content occasionally as ideas occur to him, or he may organize it as a regular feature. If the latter, it would probably be a matter for the attention of the planning conference.

Stories of public recognition of an organization give the

member a hint as to the essential value of the group. He likes to hear, also, stories of members who are outstanding in some way and reflect credit on the organization. In both instances the editor should take care that such stories have a wide geographical spread and deal with people at every level of the club life.

Planners of content hope that all such features will encourage the reader to feel glad that he is a member.

PROGRAM OF THE PARENT BODY. Some organizations have a centrally planned and administered program which is supported by local units. This is true of lodges, clubs, and religious bodies. In these cases, an organization's magazine is a main line of communication between the central office and the individual members. A good portion of its content therefore will be devoted to educating its constituency respecting various aspects of this program. Included will be features that are factual and informative, reporting work accomplished and possibly indicating future needs, and features that are interpretive and inspiring, underlining results and values. If, for example, an organization supports a children's home, a story might deal with the point of view of a recently employed director, or head resident, explaining what his plan of operation is, or it might explain the financial situation of the institution, or it might tell about some of the children in a way that emphasizes human interest. It almost goes without saying that such content is deliberately planned to involve the reader as much as possible in the institution. It also goes without saying that the editor makes sure this is done honestly and realistically, without recourse to underhand or manipulative techniques.

Some organizations also sponsor programs that are carried out locally. These can be thought of as things they hope each chapter "will do this year" or during some other stated period. These goals, as they are often called, are usually agreed upon by a body representative of the local units and channeled through a central office. They may be study programs of some sort, or service projects, or both. The content of the magazine may interpret these goals and make practical suggestions for achieving them.

At this point some words of caution are essential. Content on "message" and on "program," no matter how significant, can be designated as promotional. In other words, it is trying to sell the reader something. This is quite legitimate because it is no doubt something the reader has a prior interest in. But, and here is the caution, promotional content can be overdone. It is too easy to oversell the reader. He usually has a low tolerance for promotional material. In planning content, therefore, care must be taken to keep the promotion within bounds, limiting it to the degree and kind which the reader will readily receive and keeping it to moderate proportions in any one issue of the magazine.

In most circumstances it is the editor of the magazine who will be able to feel with his readers in this matter. Other staff members of the organization can be expected to be so involved in and committed to "message" and "program" that they are not conscious when the saturation point has been reached in promotional content. Although the editor must be aware of and sympathetic with the claims of promotional items, he must at times put up defenses and insist that other types of content, especially those based on the interests and needs of readers, will have equal if not more reader appeal. The executive officer of the organization should protect the editor in this view. With proper interpretations and attitudes of good faith, no conflict on this issue should arise within the planning group.

❖ CRITERIA OF CONTENT

The editorial planning group needs and should develop criteria for its work. There are objective standards which may be used in planning and by which the content of the magazine can be measured. The editor, as was pointed out earlier, should take the initiative in getting the group to think about these criteria. The major ones are considered in the following sections.

BALANCE. For any magazine there is the possibility of a large number of suitable subjects for content. Not every subject will appeal in equal measure to every reader. Some readers will be very much interested in a subject that will appeal hardly at all to other readers. But each section of the readership should be taken into account in planning. Most of the content will be designed for a broadly based appeal—that is, for the largest number of readers. In addition, some of the content should be explicitly directed toward one or more of the minority groups within the constituency. Some types of features can be thought of as the perennially popular, the sure-fire topics. A liberal portion of these features is advisable, but a content made up exclusively of such matter will begin to misfire. An editorial criterion, then, is balance of interests.

Here is another area in which the editor uses his understanding of his readers. He knows that in general they exhibit
some common characteristics; and he also knows that they
are not all alike. It is smart editorial policy not to treat them
as if they were. If he does not provide content that feeds the
uncommon interests of readers as well as the common ones,
he comes up with a book that is all on a dead level of unifor-
mity. Balancing the interests of his readers makes for live-
liness and zest.

COMPREHENSIVENESS. Content should not only be bal-
anced, it should also be comprehensive. The alert editor and
his planning group will explore all the possible angles of
reader interest. It is only normal that each of these persons
will tend to plug his private enthusiasms and suggest content
along those lines. This is a legitimate part of their function,
but it cannot be relied upon altogether, for it will inevitably
produce a book that is one-sided or partial.

The editor will ask such questions as: What are the pros-
pects for subject matter we are overlooking? What is happening in the experience of our readers that suggests new kinds of
content? Is there any difference in the lives of our readers
now as compared to this time last year? What are the
emergent issues for them? The answers may turn up whole
new areas for content and will keep your magazine abreast of
your people. This is one method by which comprehensiveness is achieved.

Another method is to study at regular intervals who your
readers are. They may not remain the same from one year to
the next. If your constituency parallels the membership of

your organization, how many of them are new members? If a considerable number, what features could have particular reference to them? What is the turnover in your readership? How many people have been reading your book for five years? Who are the people who stay by you, and what percentage do they bulk in the total readership? To get comprehensiveness, you take into account all your readers and you know who they are.

You also take into account the people you wish to enlist as readers and address some of the content to them. The club magazine is often a good instrument for recruiting new members, as its contents reflect the general character of the organization and give a likely prospect an idea of its principles and programs. Used in that way, the book must not assume that all its readers are active and devoted members with long experience of participation.

It is in attaining comprehensiveness that the editor uses his ability to think beyond his readers. For this reason he should not be identified with any section of his readership. This is particularly important for the editor of the house organ, who should not take on the coloration of any status group in the organization.

VARIETY OF SUBJECT MATTER AND TREATMENT. At first glance this criterion seems very much like comprehensiveness, and it is. But the difference lies in the fact that comprehensiveness applies to areas of content, whereas variety applies to the way the areas are treated. It has to do with methods of developing specific features. A single area of content would comprehend a variety of topics, methods of devel-

opment, and approaches. An editorial, a standing department, a picture-story, a report a full-dress article are ways of
treating any number of topics within an area.

The use of various styles of treatment or development is
one way to keep necessary promotional items from palling on
the reader. It is also a way in which important areas of content may be repeated. Sometimes it is necessary to tell something to the readers more than once. Try not to do it in the
same way all the time.

It is possible, of course, to overdo variety, to strain for the
new and the different. Whenever the treatment—or the way
in which a feature is handled—obscures or overshadows what
the feature has to say, communication has been thwarted. A
too-tricky layout, an elaborate handling of a fairly simple
topic are instances of technique getting in the way of purpose, of means superseding ends.

SUITABILITY TO SLANT. Reference has been made so many
times to the fact that content must be appropriate to the slant
of the magazine that it is necessary here merely to mention it
as an important criterion. Each item of content should be
subjected to the rest: Is this *our* angle in this area? Another
way of asking the same question is: Would this feature go better in another type of book our people read?

PRINCIPLES OF EFFECTIVE COMMUNICATION. Each item of
content should be planned so that it says what you want it to
say. Visually and textually it must express your meaning in
such a way as to communicate very nearly the same meaning
to your readers. What will this article say to the readers? Will
it say something you do not intend? Will it have overtones

for your readers that you are not aware of? Will its over-all impression cancel or negate what the words say?

To be communicative, a feature must also be accessible to the reader. He must be able to get rather quickly the main point. If he has to labor through a lot of text or pore over pictures closely to get at the central idea, he will be slow to comprehend. This means the article, or whatever, is inaccessible. The editorial note at the beginning of a story is often used to help the reader to arrive at the big idea and to encourage him to read the text—in other words to simplify the reader's job and make the content more accessible.

The test of communication is applied to each item of content and to any issue as a whole. The entire magazine should impress the reader as being persuasive, congenial, and directed to him in terms he understands.

❖ *LIMITS OF PLANNING*

In summary, let us say that the function of a planning group is to explore the possibilities of content consistent with policy and to decide upon the main features of all kinds to be published during a specified period of time. This is a basic task of great importance, but it is a limited one. It remains now to discuss the limitations.

A planning group works in broad outline, not in detail. When the general idea or focus of a feature has been settled, the job of the planning group is ended. All the details are left to the editor and his staff if he has one. Perhaps at a planning conference it has been decided that a profile or biographical sketch would be a popular item. The discussion will have determined the reasons for thinking so, the possible availability of data, and perhaps the slant of the piece, especially its pertinence to the magazine's purpose or message. All the rest of the decisions about the feature—who will write it, how long it will be, how it will be illustrated, and the exact date of publication — are matters which cannot be decided at the conference because these details involve many technical factors which the planning group is not competent to handle. Moreover, to consider such details would make the job of planning too cumbersome. Thus, it is left to the editor to work up agreed-upon features.

Another kind of limitation on planning was mentioned in the first section of this chapter dealing with values of planning. Plans should not put a damper on spontaneity. There should always be a place for the unplanned, unexpected feature that looks promising. If the editor has a brainstorm all his own—and he will if he is any good—he should not be stopped from following it up just because it has not been through the planning procedure. Similarly with other members of the planning conference—their out-of-turn suggestions should be welcomed by the editor.

The editor, of course, will handle these unplanned items responsibly. If one of them is of such proportions that it would upset major decisions of the conference, the editor should obtain appropriate clearances. Otherwise he will lose the confidence of his planning group; they will conclude their work does not carry any weight with him. After these unplanned features are in print, they come under the same critical analysis as all others.

The work of the planning group should not be considered all-inclusive. It is not concerned with every single item of content, some of which, while useful in the book as a whole, are fairly inconsequential. A planning conference considers major items of content and general trends in the life of the magazine. It does not hand tool the book page by page.

❖ FINAL RESPONSIBILITY OF THE EDITOR

Nothing that has been said about long-range planning should be construed as subverting the editor's executive responsibility. It should be clear to all that his is the final word on the magazine. The planning group is responsible for ideas and suggestions, without which the magazine might well be impoverished. And the editor takes these suggestions seriously, not only because they are worth taking seriously, but also because he and his planning group have a common purpose. His book is but one instrument for fulfilling that purpose.

On the other hand, the planning group is not a voting and authorizing body to whom the editor is responsible. Therefore the decisions of a planning conference are suggestive and voluntary, not mandatory. It may be that when the editor begins to work out the specific suggestions, he will find that some alterations or substitutions are necessary. In each case these are decisions for him to make. If it develops that considerable changes in plans are made, he should report the situation fully at the next conference, a procedure that will benefit everybody.

The main reason for thus preserving the final responsibility of the editor is that the job of editing a magazine is ultimately a creative and personal one. A committee, or any group, while it may function in a creative capacity, cannot bring into being the ultimate product. That must be the result of the imagination, energy, and skill of one person. His is the task of bringing together all the lines of effort and weaving them into a consistent and harmonious whole. Such is the work of the editor, and he must have the freedom necessary for such work to be accomplished.

CHAPTER TWO

PROCURING MANUSCRIPTS

In the planning conference, as we have seen, many good ideas for content will be agreed upon and will be duly noted by the editor. This brings him to the next step in the editorial process, that is, following through these suggestions and procuring the features planned. This particular job requires considerable resourcefulness on the editor's part. It involves discovering the needed contributors and often developing them to the point where they can write acceptably for his market. The editor must keep alert for possible writers and maintain a wide range of contacts.

This chapter points out the different kinds of writers who may be useful to the small magazine, beginning with the editor himself, and describes ways of obtaining their best work. It also discusses reading and judging manuscripts and handling the manuscript budget.

In practically every small magazine the editor produces some of the copy at his own typewriter, but the amount of writing he must do depends more or less on the kind of periodical he is editing and its purpose. If your book is of small proportions—say, a monthly of four typewriter-size pages (8½ x 11 inches) or eight pages of the size to fit a long business envelope (3½ x 8 inches)—and your readers are centrally located, it is a good idea to do most of the writing yourself. This is the situation of the small employee publication, or the organ of a *local* organization, even though it may be one branch or unit of a national group. The interests of such a readership will be very specialized and narrowly focused. It may be that you know many of the readers personally; even if you do not, you have a chance to make the book quite personal or even intimate in content and approach. Also the quantity of writing required each month is not so much that you would soon become "written out" or stale. You are in a better position to get the facts and other material required than anyone else, and indeed you would have to spend as much time, or more, in finding and coaching someone else in an assignment as in doing it yourself. But perhaps the chief reason for the editor to do most of the writing is that this kind of book, because of its relatively insubstantial feel and appearance, needs a striking personality to get attention. It is usually easier for one person to achieve consistency and taste in a sharp and distinctive small-magazine formula.

As soon as you get out of the class of the local, the intimate, and the simple, as soon as the periodical looks to the reader like a magazine and not a bulletin, you have a different situation. For example, in a 16-page pocket-size monthly the body of content is larger and therefore more varied. You have more kinds of features. This is even more the case if the book is a weekly or fortnightly. In fact, a weekly publication even of slender size is a fairly large operation.

Obviously in the case of a bigger book, there are more editorial chores to perform. These will take the major part of the editor's time, and he will not be able also to produce all the copy. A general working principle, therefore, can be established: the more substantial the magazine, the less writing can be expected of the editor. Accordingly, he must look elsewhere for copy. There are two obvious sources. One or more people can be added to his staff or he can find contributors outside the editorial office.

❖ STAFF WRITING ON SMALL MAGAZINES

A second person on the staff of the magazine will free the editor either from some of the routines of the process or from some of the writing assignments. The way in which these responsibilities are divided depends somewhat upon personal preference and competence. It means, however, that the major part of the book's content is staff-written. This is a good plan when the readership is tightly knit, as in the case of most employee publications. When all the readers work in one place and for a single institution—a large department store, a big university, a local manufacturing plant, the home office of a business such as an insurance company—they assume some characteristics of the family. The publication is an inside operation concentrating on features about the organization's program, policy, and personnel. This writing can only be done by the staff. Even when the book is staff-written it would be desirable to devise ways to obtain reader-contributions. Let's examine some of these ways now, keeping in mind that the same principles and techniques apply to all instances of this kind and not just to the employee publication.

Some participation by the readers is always healthy for a magazine because it enhances their feeling of proprietorship and sustains their interest. One of the common methods is a "Letters" department. Although this would be hardly appropriate in a periodical of a more or less "family" environment, it may be possible to make an adaptation that would stimulate reader-contributions. The editor might develop a department such as "Our Own Soapbox," to which he would invite contributions from readers, possibly suggesting topics in which a majority of his readers might be expected to be interested and to have opinions. These topics should be germane to the common experience of the readership, that is, "inside" topics, rather than topics in general. Some of them might be controversial, or at least topics on which people have differing views, although care should be taken that bad feeling is not generated. Such topics as the following would be suitable: My Story on the Flood, or the Hurricane, or the Traffic Tie-up, or any unusual and dramatic experience shared by the readers; I Remember When ————— (especially for long-time employees to tell something of interest from the history of the organization); Why I Don't Like ————— (a subject on which most people agree, in order to get interesting minority views, as Daylight Saving Time, or A Summer Vacation); subjects pertaining to a change or innovation in the institution, such as a move, or the remodeling of a building, or the installation of new machines; My Worst Glorious Fourth, or Most Disappointing New Year's Eve.

The editor must decide whether to publish all contributions, or only those he considers "best." There are advantages either way. If the department is very successful it is sure to pull more letters than can be printed. An announced word limit will allow space for more items. If it gets off to a slow start the editor can invite individuals to contribute who he believes have something to say.

Another method of enlisting reader participation is in news or personals, usually sent in by departments through appointed reporters. This kind of feature, though commonly found in magazines serving an institution or a company, is likely to be the dullest in the book. It is usually justified on the basis that it gets names in the publication, which is properly considered a good thing. But that is not enough. A smart editor will find ways to make this column readable. One such is to pick the reporters himself so as to get people who show at least some promise, and then to give them informal training in their job. They should understand, for example, that personals should have news value, that is, they should be interesting to people beyond the person involved and his friends, who already have the information anyway. The fact that Susan went to her brother's wedding over the week end is not an item to appeal to the general reader. But the fact that Susan has been elected state president of the Business and Professional Women would interest quite a wide range of readers. If John has a new Ford it is not news, but if he has the first Italian sports car in town it is. Not many people care to read that the president of the company has left town on a routine business trip, but if he has gone to Washington to serve on a citizens' committee of some kind, they would like to read about it.

And reading *about* it is just what they like, not merely the bare statement of fact. Reporters therefore should be trained to *write a story*, even though it may be brief, not just to turn in an item. This means that the personal items will be fewer but more interesting and the column more appealing. The fact that not so many names appear should not disturb the editor, because there are other ways of featuring individuals and groups in the organization.

It may happen that one or more of these reporters shows a nice talent for his job, in which case he could be encouraged to branch out with more ambitious assignments than personals. In any case, the editor should work closely with these people, not allowing them to settle into an automatic routine. In this way he improves the quality of his book and insures a higher degree of reader interest and participation.

❖ STAFF WRITING ON LARGE MAGAZINES

Let us consider now the situation of the publication which serves a wider and less localized constituency. In this classification fall the journal of a nation-wide institution, the house organ of a business with several branches, and the magazine of an organization with many local units. The readers will show much more diversity than in the situations described above, and they will have less in common. The sponsoring body is probably large and its operations and program complex. For these reasons the book will be substantial and somewhat formal. The 32- or 48-page monthly in a format 8½ x 11 inches, or somewhat larger, is common here.

In this situation, a major part of the content having to do with the "message of the magazine" or the "program of the parent body" should be staff-prepared. This would include stories on organization-wide events, program, and policy and on national figures in the institution. Although much of the information may come from outside his office, the editor will have the journalistic touch to develop it into appropriate magazine features. In fact, the editor and his assistants should study how to present such material persuasively, because much of it will be promotional in character. This is fundamentally a selling job and one in which the proven techniques of communication may be employed to advantage. It goes without saying that the editor works closely with the other staff members of his organization when preparing copy of this kind.

Other types of material may also be staff-written. There is the journalistic tradition that the editor write an editorial for each issue. But this tradition should be examined in the light of the purpose of the book. An editorial is always the direct and personal word of the editor to his readers. It may serve one of several functions. For example, it may express a point of view on a subject of interest to the readers. This type of editorial, on first thought, would seem to be suitable for the specialized magazine, as one means of expressing its message. However, it would not be the editor's personal word so much as the voice of the sponsoring body. This fact weakens the character and the impact of the editorial. It is less personal, and in a sense is only what the reader expects. Editorial material of this sort might better be published in a signed column of comments prepared possibly by the executive officer of the organization or the president, especially if the latter is a volunteer, that is, not on the employed staff. This plan makes the voice definitely official, and gives a leader of the sponsoring body a proper outlet.

The editor, on the other hand, may write in quite a different vein. His editorial may interpret some of the content of the issue or give some behind-the-scenes information about it. If well done, this can sell the book to the reader. Or he may develop the informal-essay type of editorial, but he should do this only if he is good at it. He may express his views on current topics of interest to his readers. In any case, the editor should use his editorial as a personal vehicle of expression, because only as such can it have strength. Through it, he forms a personal bond with his constituency, many of whom will look forward to his page, or column, or paragraph, from issue to issue.

Some very capable editors are not able to write good editorials. When this is true, the magazine will not suffer from the elimination of this feature. There is no need to follow a tradition just because it exists.

Contributions from readers in this large and somewhat formal book now under discussion will be handled differently from those in a local magazine. The readers are too widely dispersed to have an interest in the personal affairs of one another. Therefore a personals column is not appropriate and should not be attempted. There is a place here, however, for a vigorous "Letters" department, which the editor should develop by soliciting comment on topics in which the readers may be expected to have a common interest. These topics will be quite different from those suggested for smaller magazines, because here you have a loosely rather than a closely knit constituency. Reactions to the content of the magazine represent obvious topics for "Letters," as well as suggestions to the central office on the program and policy of the organization. The personal story of an event shared by at least some of the readers, such as a regional sales conference, or a dealers' meeting, or an experience of the reader (customer or employee) with a product of the company. In preparing these topics, the editor uses his understanding of the way his readers are related to the sponsoring body and where their interests lie in this relationship. Creative imagination can prime the pump on a "Letters" page and keep it going.

Stories from reporters for branches or local units are another type of reader-contribution. The number of such reporters will depend almost entirely on the size of the organization. If the number of local units is very large, it is impractical to have a reporter from each one. Perhaps a reporter from a state or region could send stories of events, trends, opinion, and the like from branches in his area. A report from each branch, or area of local units, should appear in every issue of the magazine. These "what's happening with us" stories should reflect the life of the organization—its activities, achievements, growth, perennial and short-term interests. They will tell more about the things the people concerned do together than what one individual does, except in

extraordinary circumstances. They will be sure also to deal
with content that is significant and not trivial, and that has a
wider-than-local interest.

The editor should cultivate these reporters, coaching them
in recognizing the kind of story appropriate for the magazine,
knowing how to keep in touch with news sources, and understanding how to tell the facts properly. Even so, a considerable amount of rewriting may be necessary. The copy received may contain the right information but may not be in
shape for publication. It would then be an editorial job to organize the material, to select the angles and details of widest
appeal, and to write the story in a readable style. In other
words, the editor, or someone on the magazine staff, would
use an understanding of the readers and journalistic skills that
the reporters may not possess.

If possible, the editor should know his reporters personally
and arrange for them to get together at least once a year for
training and mutual stimulation. Such a plan requires, of
course, a budget item, but the expenditure justifies itself in
the enhanced reader appeal of the magazine and reader involvement in it. Careful attention to such values often makes
the difference between a routine book that members or employees discard after a first glance and one that they read.

❖ NONSTAFF WRITERS

There remains now on any sizable magazine a large and
varied content which must come from outside the editorial
office. The editor procures this content from many sources.

MEMBERS AND STAFF OF THE ORGANIZATION. As a source

of content these other members of the parent body are next in line to the editorial staff. When the editor has an assignment that requires some inside experience or know-how, he looks around for this kind of person who is also a writer of reasonable competence. This person does not have to be a professional author, but he should possess a degree of journalistic skill. For example, on an anniversary, an article on some aspect of the history of the organization or on one of its founders or other person prominent in the early days may be wanted. It is wise policy to cultivate a small number of such people who can handle assignments of this kind. The editor can help them improve their craft through proper guidance.

STAFFS OF RELATED INSTITUTIONS. These people are only once removed from your operations, and contact may be established by exchange arrangements with other periodicals. Think of the other companies, clubs, or institutions that run somewhat parallel to yours. Each is almost sure to have a magazine with which you should be familiar. Write and offer to exchange publications. This means that each puts the other on his complimentary list of subscribers. It works the same way even if your book or theirs is given away. Through these exchanges you will receive a number of periodicals that are similar to yours in some respects, although it is almost certain that your constituencies will not overlap.

From these books you may get many ideas both on what to do and what not to do. You can profit from their mistakes as well as their successes. You also open a relationship with other editorial offices that are much like your own. Through this contact you may find possible contributors. Note the names on the masthead and in the table of contents. These

people are operating in a field at least partly similar to yours
and usually can be expected to handle the kind of assignment
you would have in mind.

FREE-LANCE WRITERS. Beyond this point the field is wide
open and an editor must depend upon his instinct, his wide
contacts, and his alert recognition. In the first place, if you
pay for manuscripts, there are thousands of people eager to
sell you stories. These free-lance writers are only waiting for
your address, which they are not likely to know because your
magazine is not available on newsstands. Most of them will
not qualify for your market, either because of the specialized
nature of your book, or because they are more hopeful than
competent. But a good number of them will. You should
look to free-lance writers for part of your copy if the content
of your book is designed to appeal to a wide, general constituency. For example, a house organ distributed to customers
and employees has a very broad base, and therefore a large
part of its content will be general in nature, that is, not directly related to the internal affairs of the company. This is
even more true of the magazine in a popular field of interest,
such as natural history or group dynamics. Almost the only
exceptions are scholarly journals and some professional magazines where it is clear that a layman writer would not qualify.

To call your periodical to the attention of free-lance
writers, you may list it in one or more of the reputable market guides. These are published in magazines which circulate
among writers, such as *The Writer* and *Author and Journalist*. If you have never been listed, an inquiry to the editor will
bring you necessary information. The listing is free and af-

fords an opportunity for you to provide the name of your periodical, publisher, frequency of publication, rates, and kind of material desired. It is likely that after your magazine has been listed in several market guides, you will begin to receive a large number of unsolicited manuscripts. In fact, there may be a flood. Most of them, probably 95 percent, will be unsuitable, but the remaining 5 percent may be worth the wear and tear of handling all the rest. That is a decision each editor must make for himself. Sometimes in this way writers are discovered who because of special abilities can undertake assignments for you.

It should be made clear at this point that no specialized magazine is competing with commercial magazines for the services of the free-lance writer. The two are in different hemispheres of the magazine world. A few free-lance writers operate in the commercial field, but most of them do not. This does not mean they are not competent or even brilliant writers. Unless your rates are unreasonably low or your content very specialized, they are interested in your market. Thus, the smart editor builds up a stable of authors who can handle, on a free-lance basis, various types of writing. One will be good on reporting, another on think-pieces, another on research, another on biography, another on the personal-experience story. These people, when they have learned your slant—and all professional authors for magazines know how to judge slant, and tailor their writing to fit—will be able to suggest their own assignments. This is what you want, because writers nearly always do a better job of developing their own ideas than yours.

THE EDITOR'S WIDER CONTACTS. Another way of finding

writers for your magazine is simply keeping your eyes and ears open. A good part of an editor's job lies outside the editorial sanctum. The reflection and pondering out of which idea-content is derived is not always a desk routine. It ripens in the back of your mind, no matter what you may be doing, and some of your best notions on content or guesses on authors may come to you while listening to a speech, or talking to a stranger on a plane, or participating in a committee meeting. In all of your contacts everywhere, not just those associated with your job, there is the possibility that you will find people who can do one or more writing jobs for your book. Keep this question turning over in your mind: What does this person know that my readers would be interested in? An editor of an employee publication said that he got a good article on "Anticipating Retirement" from a psychiatric social worker with whom he was associated in a local community chest campaign.

The possibility that a prospective writer may be almost anywhere suggests that you should "get around" to some extent, first in your local community, and then, if your magazine serves a wider readership, in many other places as well. Be alert to what is going on as reflected in events and in books and magazines. Discover people who are doing things which will be making news, and figure out if they have any relation to your readers.

All contributors who come out of your noneditorial contacts will not be professional writers. The ones who are not will usually be able to do at least one good piece in the field of their specialty, provided it is suited to your magazine.

Here is another place where some rewriting on your part may be necessary.

✣ ESTIMATING A WRITER'S COMPETENCE

On this point there is a difference between the professional and nonprofessional writer.

In the case of the latter, you judge not so much on the basis of his writing as on his familiarity with a subject. Indeed, his knowledge will usually be the reason he is being considered. But further, you must decide whether he can treat his subject in a way to appeal to or communicate with your readers. From the point of view of the magazine editor, the trouble with specialists is that they often can communicate in their field only with other specialists. They are unable to judge angles that would interest laymen and to discard the technical jargon to which they are accustomed. In other words, they know the subject matter but not your readers. Therefore, you must be sure that a prospective contributor has a clear idea of the aspects of his specialty that will interest your readers and knows that the piece must be written in layman's language. You can give him this information in face-to-face conversation, or by letter, or both. It frequently happens that such experts, although highly literate people, are not versed in the craft of magazine writing and therefore need much more guidance from you than a professional would require. Also it may be necessary to give him more time (a longer deadline) and more encouragement.

Sometimes in an initial conversation or exchange of correspondence when you are feeling out the situation, you can tell by the response you get whether or not this person will be able to fulfill your requirements. If you think not, you can either withdraw or suggest that the article be written on the basis of an interview. The interview could be handled by yourself or be assigned to a professional writer. In the previous chapter, an article was suggested on the technics of air conditioning. Here is an illustration of a feature which might be written by an expert, that is, an engineer, but which also might be developed as an interview.

Another kind of nonprofessional writer is the one who is beginning a writing career, and therefore aspires to, but has not yet reached, professional status. You will meet numbers of his kind through unsolicited manuscripts and in your mail. His manuscript itself or the letter he writes will usually reveal that he is a beginner. Whether or not you want to do any business with such writers depends entirely on your magazine and on your own inclinations. Many of them have a lot of talent, and they are using an accepted way to break into the magazine field. Obviously they cannot make the highly professional commercial-magazine market, and they believe the specialized-magazine market to be less stringent. And it is. If at times such a beginner impresses you as promising for your needs, it is to your mutual advantage for you to give him encouragement and some training in how and what to write for your market. If, then, he shows he can learn and can follow your suggestions, both of you have made a profitable contact. If he does not make such a showing, you are not obligated to continue any negotiations.

These negotiations are time-consuming, and therefore you must beware of taking on too many nonprofessionals. You must also not let your kind heart cloud your editorial judgment. It does no service to a hopeful beginner to give him encouragement that his work does not justify.

The situation is somewhat different in the case of the professional writer. Here you have his past writing to guide you in making a decision. You will decide not on competence in general but in the light of a specific assignment. What does his past performance tell you? An author may be able to do some research on facts and figures and dress them up into a first-rate article, but may not be able to handle an interview. Another may know how to describe a technical process with a high degree of popular appeal, but may not be able to write a biographical sketch. Accordingly you ask not just whether he is a good writer but whether he can make a good thing of this particular piece.

A writer may do well on ideas of his own but might be inclined to bungle an assigned subject. This is usually due to the fact that he has little initial enthusiasm for it or that he does not have the imagination to see the possibilities of the assignment. Part of the editor's responsibility is to fit the subject matter to the writer as far as he can and then try to communicate his own enthusiasm. Sometimes the author's attitude toward an assignment tips you off as to whether he will turn it out well. If he treats it too casually, this may indicate that he will write the piece carelessly, "off the top of his head." You will be wary about trying him again.

You should, of course, judge a prospective writer on the basis of his familiarity with the subject matter. A good writer on a topic he already has at hand is a natural combination. It is not, however, an essential one. Part of a writer's job is to accumulate information on topics new to him. In fact, a professional writer is skilled in doing just that, and he may even write a better piece than the nonprofessional who is an expert on the subject. He will know the angles that will interest your readers and therefore the kinds of questions to ask. He will know the sources—printed materials as well as people—from which he can get the answers.

Many of the ideas for content suggested in the previous chapter are of the kind that you would assign to a professional author who in your opinion could do it best. Sometimes the place where the writer lives is a factor in this decision. Your manuscript budget may or may not be scaled to paying travel and other expenses incurred in writing assignments. In any case, if your sources of subject matter are widespread, and they usually are when a magazine's constituency is scattered, you should try to locate free-lance writers in the main centers of your organization or activity in your field. It is a mistake to have them concentrated in the locality of your editorial office.

❖ NEGOTIATING AN ASSIGNMENT

When you have matched up your idea for an assignment with an appropriate author, you then have the sometimes crucial task of letting him know your specifications. The manner in which you do this will either help or frustrate the writer in carrying out his assignment properly. You should give him the following information in as clear-cut a fashion as you can:

1. *The general subject.* Not a title, but a descriptive phrase or even sentences that indicate the contemplated content of the article, for example, "good techniques for chairing a committee and for conducting a business session." This description should indicate also the reason that you think your readers will be interested in the subject, which will help the writer decide on emphases and approach.

2. *The approximate length.* Usually given in number of words. This is vital information, because it determines the amount of detail or the number of fine points the article may contain. The editor decides on length in the light of the nature of the topic and weight it will carry in the book. The example above would probably have medium weight—that is, not as much as a story on a national project of the organization, but more than a report on a local activity. This subject could probably be handled adequately for this purpose in eighteen hundred words.

3. *The deadline.* The date you want to receive the finished manuscript. You suggest a deadline that will allow the author reasonable time (but not so much that his first enthusiasm for the assignment will fade) and that will allow the article to be scheduled at a time convenient to you. The writer may suggest an alternative date that suits his work better, which the editor should accept if he can. Your purpose is to get a good article; making things as right as possible for the author is just common sense. Free-lance writers will have other assignments, and except in extraordinary circumstances you

should not expect immediate work. A month is usually a reasonable amount of time. Assignments that require more work, for example, the beginning of a series, will naturally require a longer deadline.

4. *The fee.* The fact that an author is a professional usually means that he makes all or a part of his living by his typewriter. Tell him exactly what you are prepared to pay. The fact that he is concerned about payment does not mean that he is mercenary or that he is not interested in doing a good job. He will do a better job if he feels adequately paid.

5. *Possible sources of information.* Sources of information you think the writer needs to know, or any advice you can give on getting the necessary facts.

You can make manuscript solicitations by telephone—local or long-distance—telegraph, or mail. Using the telephone makes it possible to get a quick answer, which is sometimes an advantage to you. However, if arrangements are made by telephone, or by telegraph, they should always be confirmed by letter.

Clear and definite specifications go far to insure the successful handling of an assignment. These same specifications are given by the editor even if the assignment was originated by the author. Although there may have had to be more consultation about the assignment, the agreement between the editor and the author should be made formal. Also, the editor may suggest in the specifications certain angles on a general topic proposed by the author.

When an editor makes an assignment and it is accepted by an author, it is necessary for the editor to know how far he has committed himself to accept the completed manuscript.

The fact is that when the editor takes the initiative in asking a writer to do a job and has confirmed the invitation with a letter of specifications, he has made a contract that is legally binding. This means that he has committed himself to accept the manuscript. Only when the author clearly has not conformed to specifications could this contract be broken.

Therefore, in any substantial assignment the editor works with the writer to help him turn out an acceptable job. For example, the writer may submit an outline of the piece on which the two confer. It is standard practice for the editor to request an outline or a rough first draft of part of a long manuscript, so that he can check to see whether he and the author understand the specifications in the same way. A writer may easily misconstrue the editor's wishes. Conferring at this stage guards against drastic revisions at a later stage, after the author has done a lot of work. It is standard practice, however, among professional writers to offer to revise a manuscript even after it is completed to make it more acceptable. In other words, it is mutually beneficial for an editor and author to cooperate in bringing work in line with specifications. Of course, in their consultation it may happen that the writer will suggest changes that are quite agreeable to the editor. The editor should be conscientious in not requiring an unreasonable amount of revision. For example, he should not change his mind after an author has fulfilled his part of an agreed-upon plan.

The editor may, nevertheless, receive a final draft which he considers not acceptable. Several things may account for this unfortunate circumstance. The author may have done his best but still have fallen short of the editor's expectations.

This usually means that the editor showed unsound judgment either in his selection of the subject—maybe it wasn't a fruitful idea in the first place—or in his choice of an author. Perhaps the author has simply turned out a poor piece of writing. Regardless of the reason, the editor is obligated to pay for the manuscript. However, he is not obligated to publish it, and he should not do so. It is unreasonable to expect every assignment to turn out successfully. On the other hand, an editor who has a high percentage of failures is not handling his job in the best way.

The situation is different when an author suggests his own assignment. Here he is working on speculation and will expect to be paid *only* for an acceptable manuscript. Even when an editor agrees that a proposed idea sounds promising, he should make it clear that he is not committing himself in advance. Any letter that he writes about the proposal should state that fact clearly. With writers whom he does not know, he should, in order to be fair, agree to their going ahead only when he thinks there is a good chance that the work will be acceptable. If the writer is one whose work is accepted with some regularity, the editor can afford to be really encouraging.

Whereas rewriting in the editorial office is to be expected on manuscripts from various kinds of nonprofessional contributors, it should not be necessary in the case of professional writing. If you find that you are tempted to rewrite every manuscript, something is wrong. Perhaps your book is so specialized that people not in your field cannot hit your slant or handle your subject matter. Or perhaps your content is so "internal," that is, so intimately tied in with your group or organization, that "outsiders" cannot really get your point of view. If that is true, most or even all of your content should be staff-prepared. On the other hand, it is possible that your specifications are too rigid. You may be expecting a manuscript to turn out as you would have written it. That is usurping the writer's responsibility. An editor must always remember that the manuscript is the author's work and that the writer must be free to do it in his own style and with his personal flair. Nothing that has been said about specifications should be interpreted to mean an author's creativity should be curbed. The editor's job is to stimulate and release the author's energy and imagination, not to put him in a strait jacket.

✤ UNSOLICITED MANUSCRIPTS

The great majority of manuscripts you handle will be those that arrive in the mail unsolicited. Sometimes a considerable amount of clerical work is required in connection with these manuscripts. As was indicated above, however, this is necessary and even advantageous if you use work of free-lance authors.

CLERICAL ROUTINES. You must first of all establish a system of recording manuscripts in and out. A good way is to set up a card file on which the history of each manuscript is permanently recorded. The card for each manuscript should show the author's name and address, the title, a description of any enclosures (for example, 3 photographs), the date it was received, and its disposition—either "returned" with rejection slip or letter and the date, or "accepted" and the date, plus the amount paid. It may also be useful to note whether or not return postage was included when the manuscript was submitted.

Manuscripts should be stored in a clean, safe place until they have been read and disposed of. Most of them, including their return envelopes, will fit conveniently into a letter-size file drawer. Although no editorial office is responsible for unsolicited manuscripts, it is only fair to the authors that good care be taken of their manuscripts. Most authors dislike having paper clips used on their manuscripts. If you must use clips, be sure they do not tear or mark the sheets.

You should read and return manuscripts within two weeks, or at most one month. A longer time is discourteous and will prompt letters of inquiry from their authors, which must be answered—this would be an addition to the editorial routine.

A big majority of the unsolicited manuscripts will be returned with a rejection slip. This slip should be not larger than 3½ x 6 inches in order to fit a small business envelope and should be printed on paper, not a card. The wording of the rejection should be dignified and firm but not uncordial. The following statement would be suitable: "We thank you for submitting your manuscript and regret that we do not find a place for it in our plans." The name and address of your magazine should appear at the top. It is the accepted practice among authors to enclose with their manuscripts a stamped, self-addressed envelope, or at least return postage, but occasionally a manuscript arrives without either. You are not obligated to return such a manuscript, but you may send it back in one of your own envelopes and type on the rejection slip: "Be sure to enclose return postage." Or you may send a postal card saying the manuscript will be returned on receipt of postage. If you receive no reply after a reasonable length of time, you are justified in destroying the manuscript. Editorial offices, as was said above, are in no way responsible for unsolicited manuscripts. The manuscript card, of course, remains on file. The history of solicited manuscripts should similarly be recorded, but the reading routine may be different; that is, they may receive special handling.

READING MANUSCRIPTS. The size of your operation and the number of your staff will determine whether more than one person reads all the unsolicited manuscripts. Unless your book is large enough to require more than one person with editorial (not clerical or secretarial) duties, the editor himself will be the sole reader. On his judgment returns and acceptances will be made, although occasionally he will request an opinion of another interested person.

The editor may assign to an assistant the duty of giving the manuscripts a first reading, of sending back all the "impossibles," and of referring to the editor only those which show some possibility. This assistant should note his opinions of manuscripts which he passes on to the editor.

What do you look for as you plow your way through the piles of manuscripts? How do you read them?

First, you are looking for content that is lively, timely, and appropriate for your book. Here your imagination comes into play in much the same way as in the process of planning. Does the big idea or the pertinent facts in this piece say anything significant and relevant to your readers? Will it help to further the purpose of your magazine respecting your readers? Watch for some of the common failings such as the encyclopedia rewrite, which no one cares about; the once-over-lightly job, which reveals that the author has approached his subject superficially, has not dug deeply for the really interesting facts; the obvious subject that is always thought of first; the hackneyed theme; the article that answers questions no one is asking.

Second, you are looking for skillful communication. Assuming the subject matter is what you want, observe the way it has been developed. Recall what was said on communication in Chapter 1 and ask: Is the writing clear? Are the sentences lucid? Do you grasp quickly what the author is saying? The sentences should be straightforward and simple in construction. Even long sentences are readable if the structure is apparent and can be readily followed. Notice style and diction. Adjectives should not overbalance verbs. The verb moves and activates a sentence; it says to the reader that something happened. Does the style draw pictures and call up mental images through specific and graphic details? Or does it depend on vague and generalized statements? Has the writer personalized the content, showing how it matters to people, especially to those reading your magazine? Does the writer tell in episodes or anecdotes how individual persons have been related to the subject in any way? And finally, is the material organized so the reader can grasp its meaning quickly? Here you watch for the way the author uses the paragraph, which is the key to the structure of the article. Does one paragraph follow logically or psychologically out of the preceding one so that you keep moving in a well-defined direction? On the other hand, do you notice that the facts or

points are sprinkled through the pages without being organized into a pattern? This may be because some writers have the
mistaken idea that brevity of sentences and paragraphs, rather
than the organization of material through paragraphing,
brings about better communication.

ACCEPTING AND REJECTING. When you find an acceptable
manuscript, that is, one that at least approximates what you
are looking for, you mark it for payment and record the fact
on its file card. There are a few occasions when you might
return an acceptable manuscript: when your budget is over-
drawn so that you are not buying manuscripts; when your inventory of manuscripts is high and you do not need additions;
when the content of the piece duplicates an item already on
hand. Most of the time, however, you will feel fortunate in
discovering a good unsolicited manuscript and will be only
too glad to send a check.

Payment for manuscripts should be sent promptly, certainly not later than one month after acceptance. Any other
policy is irresponsible and asks too much of writers, who
regard a prompt check as highly as a generous one. Checks
may be processed as soon as requisitioned by the editor, or
once or twice a month, according to the general routines of
the accounting office.

Always write a letter of acceptance when you buy a manuscript. This is a pleasant chore because it is nice to be the
purveyor of good news. Tell the author what you like about
his manuscript. That will encourage him and put you to a
useful discipline. A letter is not necessary in the case of a
small routine item if the check carries a voucher explaining

the payment. In all other cases, your letter also should name the manuscript by title, mention the exact amount being paid, and state approximately the time when the author may expect his check if it is not enclosed. In addition, it should state the rights in the manuscript you are purchasing. This last point is essential, because your letter is a legal contract.

Many different rights inhere in a manuscript, all of which belong to the author. They are the rights to print it in a magazine or newspaper the first, second, or any number of times; to publish it in a book; to use it as the basis for a radio or TV show; to make it into a drama. It is not conceivable that an author can always market all these rights to every manuscript, but he and only he may do so, because he is their legal proprietor. The editor of a specialized magazine is interested usually in first serial rights, that is, the license to publish the material for the first time in a periodical. That is usually all the author is offering for sale; in fact, many times a manuscript will read in the upper right-hand corner of the first page: "First serial rights only." All other rights remain the author's property, and he may assign them as he wishes.

Some manuscripts will be the almost-but-not-quite variety which may require special handling. If the author is known to you and has sold you things in the past, you should write a letter of rejection instead of enclosing the routine slip. This is a courteous practice which helps you maintain a good relationship with your author. Tell the author in the letter as exactly as you can why you are returning his manuscript. Your best critical judgment may be required for you to decide what is wrong. Take time to think it through clearly and to tell the author plainly. Don't generalize by saying "not up to standard," but explain why: "The article does not contain enough human-interest angles." Free-lance writers testify that letters from editors are very much prized because they learn about a market from what an editor says. This applies as much to letters of rejection as to letters of acceptance. The editor also benefits because it cuts down the number of unsuitable manuscripts.

The tone of such letters is important. Keep it friendly and do not say or imply that the piece is "no good." All that you mean anyway is that it is "no good" for you. To keep a friendly tone does not mean to be encouraging about a manuscript in which you are not interested. The rejection should be firm.

It may be that you think a manuscript could be revised by the author so that it would be acceptable. If so, return it with a letter in which you propose specific revisions. Suggest that if the writer is interested he make the changes and resubmit the article. Be sure you explain these changes carefully and explicitly. Nine times out of ten, you will get the revised manuscript back almost by return mail. If the new version is not suitable, you are still not obligated to accept it. Nevertheless, you are more committed than you were when you read the piece the first time, for the writer has spent time and effort at your suggestion. It is well, therefore, not to propose a revision unless you are reasonably sure the writer can comply or unless the changes are minor. If you handle such a situation with care, you will probably be able to accept the second version without embarrassment.

One of the editor's recurring problems is the manuscript submitted by a personal friend or the friend of a colleague. When such a manuscript turns out to be acceptable, all is well. But when it does not, the difficulty of a suitable rejection is compounded by either personal friendship or public relations. "Friends" find it hard to see why their manuscripts are not as good as those you publish all the time. Do not let your good feeling for or obligation to the persons involved persuade you to go against your editorial judgment. Your rejection, however, should employ tact and resourcefulness, so that the friend does not feel you have rejected him personally. To do this requires as much thought about the person as about the manuscript.

Editors, of course, in common with all other people, are never completely objective in their judgments. Your feelings, pet prejudices, and private enthusiasms inevitably pull some weight in all the decisions you make. Even so, you should be aware of what they are and strive for as much objectivity as you can summon. Although the way your nerve ends react to a manuscript is often a reliable guide, your reaction should be supported by some solid, cold reasoning. When you must make a decision on a manuscript of some substance—a series of articles, or the launching of a regular column—it is well to let the matter simmer in your mind for a while, so as to give yourself a chance to see it from different angles and to think about it in a variety of situations. Advice from your colleagues and selected readers may be helpful. In the end, however, it must be your decision. You must feel right about it. No matter how expert the opinion of someone else, it should inform, but not supplant your editorial judgment.

❧ WRITER-EDITOR CONTACTS

Your mail will bring letters of inquiry as well as manuscripts. Writers will want to know whether you would be interested in a certain subject, and often they will describe how they expect to treat it. The letters may also include a statement of credentials. Nearly always a stamped, self-addressed envelope for reply will be enclosed. This is the situation, referred to above, where an author suggests his own assignment. It is courteous to answer such letters promptly, and extremely discourteous to ignore them altogether. Your reply should be strictly honest. The writer is not asking you to accept a manuscript sight unseen. He is asking your judgment on whether he would be wasting his effort and yours to submit the manuscript. If the subject is a suitable one and the letter makes you think the author may be able to develop it acceptably, you tell him to go ahead and submit it, on speculation of course. If the whole thing is unpromising, you send a negative reply. If it sounds very promising, you may suggest a proper slant and word length. When the manuscript arrives, as was indicated earlier, you are not obligated in any way. It receives the same critical estimate that all others receive.

These letters may open up channels for good content, and together with all of those mentioned earlier they sustain your writer-editor contacts that are important. Unless your editorial office is in a large publishing center, to which writers tend to gravitate, you will meet your contributors mainly through correspondence. Accordingly, you should give close attention to your mail and study how to write letters which will genuinely convey your meaning. They must take the place of face-to-face conversation, in which communication is nearly always easier. Some of the best writers need the kind of concrete suggestions and encouragement an alert editor can supply. Also, specialized magazines must often train writers for their market. An editor can do a lot of coaching by mail and so establish a relationship that is mutually advantageous. As was indicated earlier in this chapter, the smart editor always works to the end that a promising idea will turn out successfully, and that a promising person has a chance to fulfill that promise. He cannot shift that responsibility entirely to the writer, whether staff or nonstaff.

It is surely clear by this time that good content and good copy will not show up automatically just because your editorial sign is out.

❖ THE MANUSCRIPT BUDGET

Some small magazines do not pay for manuscripts. This is the case when the contents are staff-prepared or when they are extremely specialized and the book's circulation is very much restricted. Magazines which are run on a shoestring, often in support of a cause, generally do not pay for manuscripts. If they solicit manuscripts at all, it will usually be from persons who have an interest in the cause and will contribute their writing free.

Any specialized magazine which uses content from sources outside its group or which makes an appeal to a general constituency will require a manuscript budget. In this class are the journals of large membership organizations, such as religious bodies, federations of clubs or leagues, fraternal societies; national business, professional, and labor groups; organs of industries or business firms circulated to customers or to employees over a wide area.

There are no accepted standards on rates of payment for manuscripts. Each magazine usually decides for itself what it can afford to pay. This means that some would pay more than others for the same or a similar manuscript. Every magazine should, however, establish each year a stated sum to pay for manuscripts. Payments should not come out of a general fund of the parent body on a casual and unplanned basis. This annual amount, or budget, should then be a guaranteed allocation from the organization's resources.

The nature of the book usually determines the budget figure. A rule of thumb in establishing a budget is to calculate the average amount of content (number of words) to be purchased in any one issue and multiply it by the number of issues per year. For example, a 16-page, pocket-size monthly might include 30,000 words per year bought in the open market. A weekly of the same size would probably use about 120,000 words; a 32-page monthly of 8 x 11 inches, 240,000 words. These estimates assume that only half or a little more than half of the content is paid for, the rest being staff-prepared or not charged against the manuscript budget.

Payment for a manuscript is per word, and the budget should be set on an established, or an average, rate per word. The editor will know in general how much work a writer will have put into a 1,000-, 1,500-, or 3,000-word piece. His payment should be at least roughly commensurate with his effort. As a rule of thumb, word rate for the average piece is at present 4–5 cents a word. That would mean $65 to $75 for

1,500 words. That figure is a minimum or a floor. Several factors might make it advisable to pay more: a piece that requires a lot of research, one that makes necessary a trip by the writer (if his expenses are not paid), or one that carries special weight in your book. It is not unusual to think of $100 as a rough figure for a single item of acceptable work, and decrease or increase in accordance with the factors just listed.

It is also unnecessary to pay every author at the same rate. A promising but beginning writer with whom you have spent time and effort in "training" would receive less than a professional whose work is such that it does not require a large amount of time and effort by the editor. The rate per word is not rigid for another reason. It is harder to write a good short piece—300 words—than a long one. This is especially true when the short piece has been solicited.

In deciding on your manuscript, you should also take into account what you are paying for other services. For printing and for engraving you will of necessity pay the going rate, that is, what these strongly organized trades charge. The fact that professional free-lance writers are unorganized and operate on an individual basis means that generally you and not they decide what they should be paid. It is grossly unfair to penalize your writers for this situation.

❖ THE BUDGET

Money is allocated to be spent. The job of the editor is to spend it so as to sustain the quality of his magazine. He uses caution in his expenditures, but also imagination.

At the beginning of a fiscal year he calculates the amount of money which may be spent on manuscripts in each issue by dividing the total budget by the number of issues per year. He then may estimate the number of pages for which manuscripts will be purchased, and he arrives at a predicted cost per magazine page. This hypothetical figure may be used as one factor in deciding what to pay for a specific manuscript.

The central accounting office of the organization should furnish the editor at regular intervals a cumulative statement of his expenditures on manuscripts, by which he can judge whether or not his buying is in line with his predicted costs. If there is a sizable credit in the budget, that is, if he has not been spending on the average the amount allocated per issue, it means either that his inventory of manuscripts is low, or that he has not needed as much content as estimated, or that he is paying at a lower rate than was predicted when the budget was fixed. If there is a sizable debit, it means the reverse of one or more of these conditions. If the credit or debit continues, a new policy with respect to buying or with respect to the budget should be worked out.

The editor who is alert to his budget situation will handle his investment in manuscripts so that his spending averages out and a continued large credit or debit does not occur. It is not possible, of course, to spend in any given month exactly the estimated amount for the issue, or issues, involved. The amount of copy needed and opportunities for purchases vary from one month to another. That is the reason for an average.

Although the budget is established on the basis of a certain rate of payment, the editor does not pay at that rate invariably. There are some exceptions to the general practice. The types of nonprofessional writing described earlier in this chapter do not necessarily command professional rates. Each case must be decided on its merits. It may be a good idea to splurge on an important feature in order to vary the pace of the magazine's content, or to enlist special attention, or to give you something to shout about—all of which are ways of maintaining reader interest. Some pieces, though brief, may require very special skills. The pungent 100- to 150-word paragraph used as a regular column deserves a higher word rate than the normal informative article.

In the usual course of budget administration, there come times when you must economize. The way to save money is not to cut your rates to authors. Instead, you invent content for which there is no manuscript charge. Possibly you can think of more features to be written by the staff members of the organization or ideas that you yourself can work up for a couple of pages. Another possibility is reprints. Look at your exchanges to see whether they contain something suitable for your book. It is likely that the editor of the other book will give you permission to reprint one of his articles, a practice that is quite customary, provided his magazine owns reprint rights. You would naturally reciprocate when the situation is reversed. Also, you may request reprint permission from a commercial magazine provided it is not a mass-circulation periodical which your readers are sure to have seen. Consumer magazines do not give reprint permissions to others in their field, but they usually will do so to a specialized magazine clearly not in competition with them. Still another idea is to print a digest of a good speech. If delivered to more than two hundred people, it is in the public domain and therefore free.

Do not try to save all your money on two or three issues. Spread it out so your economizing will not show to your readers. They are not in position to know the facts, and their reaction will not be: "How clever of our editor to save money this way!" They are more likely to say: "How dull can this magazine get?"

CHAPTER THREE

PICTURES

This chapter does not deal with the subject of taking pictures but of learning to select pictures and of using them effectively in your magazine. The first part of the chapter considers photographs and the second half with ways of obtaining and using art.

In the publishing world today there are very few magazines that do not make use of photos; some use them very liberally. The reasons are not hard to find. The picture, if well used, has an immediacy of impact that text cannot claim. The picture gives an additional impression of the printed word that enhances its meaning. Pictures also grab the attention of the reader faster than the text on most pages.

The art of taking pictures and the technology of the camera have both leaped forward in the last ten years, making possible not only an expanding industry, but also a new hobby for hundreds of people.

All of the foregoing sounds very grand and possibly discouraging to the editor of a modest small magazine. But that would be a mistaken reading. What this means is that more and better use of photographs is possible for him these days simply because of this advance. Not every expert photographer is a Yoshikazu Shirakawa, who made the astounding pictures in *Himalayas,* a coffee table book to end all others!

❧ THE PURPOSES OF PICTURES

Some purposes of pictures in a small magazine have been noted above but there are other important ones. A list may be helpful.

1. To enhance the text in order that the meaning may be clearer and the reader more interested and edified. You can read a recipe or how to put together any object that arrives in pieces in a flat box, but pictures of someone actually carrying out the steps is much more profitable to you.

2. To provide additional information. The owner's manual of your new automobile with well-done diagrams certainly helps you understand better the insides of your car.

3. To establish a mood. Often effect is accomplished with one large photo expressing rage, or joy, or grief, or reflection.

4. To dress up a page and make it look more alluring to the reader, or to arouse the reader's sympathy or some other generalized emotion that gets him started on at least the first paragraph.

Some of these purposes may be combined in a single picture. Finally, a caution: Unless your piece is largely a picture book, you must be careful that the pictures do not overpower the text. After all, you hope people will *read* your magazine, and not just look at it.

❖ SOURCES OF PICTURES

Let us think first of black and white; color will come later.

Many kinds of photographers, but not all of them, are available to you and want to do business with you.

You will likely from time to time want to obtain two kinds of pictures: those already printed, of which you purchase one print for one reproduction only (more about that later); and those taken just for you. In this description of sources, both kinds are assumed.

Consider first your local community. Who takes pictures in your town? The local newspaper, preferably a daily (a weekly will not be suitable for several reasons, the main one being that most of both text and pictures originate elsewhere). Look at the photo credits. The man or men (it is almost never a woman, because of the necessity of carrying heavy equipment) will usually have some photos as private stock, and also he is almost always available for a moonlighting job that, of course, must not conflict with his working hours on the paper.

Take into account the *talented* and *experienced* amateur, no shutter bugs need apply. He should be able to do his own darkroom work. The reason is that much of the quality of a print is the result of what happens in the darkroom. An amateur may take better pictures than some professionals but he does not earn his living by it, which is the only reason to use the term "amateur," and he is likely not to be available when wanted. Also, portrait photographers are so specialized that they are not a valid source for you.

Commercial developing of prints will sometimes be necessary. Try to avoid the mass operation that is distributed through a local drug store. The work is often of poor quality and the paper used is almost sure to be inferior. Find a small concern with which you can establish the kind of relationship that allows you to make suggestions about the development of the film and the time by which you need prints.

While on the subject of the development of film, we should say something about paper, that is, the paper the film will be printed on and the paper the print will be reproduced on. It is not necessary for you to be an expert in this subject in order for you to show the print developer a copy of your magazine in order for him to judge the kind of paper used and the process by which it is printed. Be free in making such suggestions to him as "a sharper image," "less degree of dark in the print as a whole." This sort of thing used to be simple: a sharp black and white printed on glossy paper. That is still a useful requirement but there are others now. Many pictures are now developed on a matte finish paper that comes out well in reproduction and gives a softer (but not fuzzy or unfocused) appearance, which may be the effect you want. In this case the stock on which it is reproduced should be appropriate for this matte look. The mood picture mentioned earlier may take this soft look very well. Mass photo developing firms often use a cheap kind of paper that will make your pictures look a little muddy when the original prints were sharp. The reason for using this paper is that a firm can charge less for the finished prints. For candid snap shots at the family reunion that may serve well but not for reproduction in a magazine.

In contrast to the general "sharp black and white" look,

some photographers and editors today occasionally want what they call "low definition" pictures, which means that the images look slightly out of focus. The reason is the emotional appeal is often stronger than the sharp linear look.

If you are not familiar with this aspect of business, look in the yellow pages. For example, you may find two: *Creative Arts Inc.* and *Image.* That is the kind of "arty" name to look for. These firms (maybe one will be just an office) are prepared to do many kinds of services in the field, all the way from one photograph to designing your whole magazine. The quality of their work, hence their prices, vary from here to there to yonder. So be sure to examine many samples of their productions of the kind that interest you and be firm and detailed in your discussion of fees. In a small magazine perhaps such firms would be used sparingly. Prices are bound to be high but quality may be high too.

Now let us consider photographic service by mail. First, there are large or even small specialized photographic houses who use the services of many people and have huge stocks. A letter from you detailing the kind of picture(s) you want and their purposes will likely bring a package of prints on approval. The price will be standard in each case for one reproduction only. Anywhere from $10 to $15 each is not out of line. Handle the prints carefully, any smudge or scratch will show up when it is reproduced. Make your decision promptly and return the prints immediately, preferably in the kind of container they arrived in. Remember that both film and prints are sensitive to weather and atmospheric conditions. Keep both away from direct sun or high heat.

These large firms employ photographers, chiefly on a free-

lance basis, in many large cities, even overseas. So if you
want some shots of the national meeting of your dealers away
from the home office, the photo firm will suggest names.
Usually the local newspaper will, also. If you will not be
there to give him instructions about the kind of pictures you
want, write in advance and be very specific, e.g., the president, or whoever, making the keynote speech, informal shots
of the people milling around at the reception, get some wives
in somewhere. Send a copy of your magazine so he will have
some idea of how the pictures will be reproduced and used. If
you plan to be present, you make these suggestions in person.
In fact, he will look to you to tell him in the main what to
shoot.

It is always expensive to have photos made expressly for
your use. The reason is that usually a firm has no other
market for the print. In that case the price will be higher (it
usually gets less the more prints you buy). If the firm has
other possible markets, they will keep the negatives, of
course, and they become the firm's property. If they cannot
sell the prints elsewhere their fee is higher, as stated earlier,
and you retain the negatives as well as *all* the prints as your
property. This arrangement is called exclusive rights to print
the photo. More on this when we come to the legal situation
involved in reproducing pictures.

In the case we are discussing you might be able to get pictures you can use in several issues. Remember in this case
that a photographer is selling through the firm not only developed prints but his time, and the high price does not seem
then so unreasonable. You would be smart to arrange things

so that he can do as much of his shooting as possible at one session. Also, if he is shooting people, you should make sure they arrive on time and do not let them waste his time. Be firm about all these things because actually you are in charge of the situation.

Other sources of photos may be mentioned. If your publication is a fairly large operation, perhaps the magazine of a national organization, it should be able to afford a staff photographer paid a salary and presumably available to work most of the time. The magazine pays for all his equipment and supplies and furnishes darkroom facilities. "Most of the time" means he might have the same arrangement with another publisher. It's rather like a retainer for an attorney.

Then again the editor himself may be his own photographer. In case of a modest operation this is an inexpensive and usually a simple way to solve what is often a complicated problem for the small magazine.

Free photographs are usually available on request from museums, government agencies, and public relations departments of almost any organization. You explain who you are, what you want, how you will use the print(s). If what you want is available, a small packet will arrive, not always quickly. You make your selection quickly, however, and return the rest of the package. A note of appreciation is an appropriate courtesy.

Many free-lance writers send pictures with their manuscripts. If they are good and you use them, you pay for them separately from the manuscript even if it is clear the author got the photos free, as above. But you are paying him for the tedious editorial chore of getting the pictures and dealing with all the correspondence involved—in other words, his time.

❖ SPECIAL EFFECTS

In dealing with photographs, it is now possible to achieve special effects. It is good to know about them but usually they are so pronounced that the editor should use them sparingly, especially if his readers are not likely to take readily to something new and perhaps radical. Some of these treatments of film are made by the photographer when taking the picture, some are techniques employed in the darkroom, and some are produced when the layouts are being made. See Chapter 5.

We will begin with an easy one for most any photographer and one that is used a lot. Suppose you plan an article on bikes—their selection, use, and care. It is obvious that you will require pictures related to these three angles of the subject. As you think about how you want the article to look, you decide one dramatic shot would open the piece. And so you ask the photographer to make one shot showing a bike rider going very fast past the eye of the reader. He really is in motion. The photographer has made this possible by keeping his shutter open long enough for the action, not just the subject, to become a part of the picture. Of course, there will be no sharp images and this is right because when you are biking fast you do not see things in sharp focus. The function of such a photo is to make the reader think to himself "Isn't this exciting?" Then he is in the mood for the text and the more conventional informative pictures.

In the darkroom it is now possible to treat photos so that they come out looking as if they were clever black on white prints. All the grays have gone, and you see interesting black and white spaces in an artistic relation to one another. You may or may not be able to recognize the original photo, and not all photos lend themselves to this process. An imaginative editor can do a lot with one such picture.

While the film is being developed, the photographer may use a kind of stroking process that makes the finished picture look as if the object, generally a head-on single figure, were behind a transparent veil or even an erratic-looking fence.

Most of these tricky techniques (there are others you can find out about) are, naturally, very self-conscious. They will immediately call attention to themselves and should never be used if that is all they do. The editor should have a purpose beyond "the effect" itself. Also, too much use will make them less and less dramatic.

❖ WORKING WITH A PHOTOGRAPHER

Sometimes you will plan a feature in your book that is mainly pictures and captions, with not much text, if any. This sort of arrangement is often called a photo-feature, and depends upon the editor working very closely with the photographer The paragraphs below describe such an instance.

Suppose you are editing a house publication circulated to the employees of a large business. You want a picture-story about a recently established department. First, you clear the project with the head of the department, explaining the length of time required. He then advises you on a date and hour suitable for taking pictures. You make sure that he has notified all the people involved of the plan and the date; it is never a good idea to confront people without warning with a request for their picture if it is going to be published. In fact, you have no legal right to print their pictures without their permission (see the next section). It is likely that your subjects will be pleased to have their department played up in the magazine, provided the picture-taking, which should be done on company time, is scheduled so that it does not seriously interfere with the department's work.

When these arrangements have been made, you get in touch with your photographer and discuss with him exactly what you want: a complete picture-story of the department— its people and activities—with a final total of eight to twelve photographs. The photographer will take many more pictures than that, so that you will have perhaps twenty prints from which to make selections. You describe to him the operations of the department, what the various people do, and suggest some typical shots. Possibly you and the photographer agree on a process story, that is, one that begins at the beginning with a specific piece of work and carries it through all the operations. This plan has the advantages of being easy for the reader to follow and including all the workers. From the standpoint of public relations, it would be a mistake in a story of this kind to leave out any of the people involved in the department's work.

It would be wise for you to consult again with the head of

the department, and possibly with some of his staff, explaining your plan for a process story and arranging for any necessary properties. Unless you understand the operations very well, you will need the help of these people in plotting the steps in the process. The photographer may make a preliminary visit to investigate lighting and setting requirements.

On the agreed date, you accompany the photographer, make all the introductions, and tell everybody how the pictures will be used. As the photographer works, you assist in getting the right people together for each shot and in handling any little courtesies that will make them happier. The photographer will take two or more exposures of each shot and will attempt some variety of composition, taking pains to arrange it and light it properly. On an assignment of this kind, he is likely to bring along an assistant.

While the pictures are being made, you are taking notes which you will use later in writing the captions or cut lines for the pictures. You note the names of the people, with proper spelling, and anything about the subject of each picture that is not obvious from its content. All the pictures should be completed on this occasion, because you should not expect either your subjects or your photographer to go through the work more than once. This now-or-never condition means that you must take every care in advance to set up the situation properly.

In this feature, the burden of the story is carried by the pictures plus the captions, with very little accompanying text. It is really a photo-feature, which when well done makes excellent copy. The editor and photographer build the story so that its several parts hang together coherently and its story line moves toward a climax. When you select the pictures to be published from the total group of prints supplied by the photographer, you keep in mind this story structure. Also, you make sure no essential element of the story has been omitted and that the appropriate emphasis is conserved. You should not leave out one of the important steps in the process nor magnify an unimportant one. Also aim for variety in contrasting color-tone of the prints, in close and long shots, in horizontal and vertical proportions.

It is a nice gesture of appreciation to send to each person involved in a picture-story like the one here described a print of the photograph in which he appears.

❖ COLOR

In Chapter 6, various kinds of printing processes are described. One of these is called "offset." When first introduced, offset represented the culmination of many years of experimentation by publishers and printers to find a better method of getting ink on coated paper. Better and cheaper, one might add, because the costs involved in letterpress were burgeoning alarmingly with little hope for quick relief.

Offset printing was the answer. One of its fortuitous byproducts was the ease with which the process could produce high-quality four-color reproduction. Use of color with letterpress printing had been prohibitively costly. Now, it was not only practical and reasonably priced; it was also widely available as the competition among printers mounted. Today, offset printing accounts for about 85% of all published material in the nation. No wonder, then, the wide use of color in American publications.

At present, color photography is very popular. Almost everyone who snaps a shutter wants his film developed in either color prints or slides. Probably it was the first motion picture in color that started this trend, assisted by magazine ads. The black and white magazine is getting lost under the barrage of a maximum and sometimes bizarre use of color in the magazine world.

Most people realize that there is a big and expensive difference between color and black and white photography. They know this even if they do not know the differences in film techniques and the development of film. It was not so long ago that all color film had to be sent to Rochester to be developed because Eastman controlled the process. The patent situation has changed so that often color film may now be developed locally. The reason for the expense was the making of color plates used in letterpress printing.

The offset process has developed a way to reduce the cost of color printing so much that color is not now beyond the budget of many small magazines. As you will see in the chapter on printing, offset is a process based on photography and does not use the same kind of costly color plates as letterpress. This fact is mentioned in this chapter because you may want to buy color pictures from your favorite photographer. What you will get is called a "transparency" mounted in a cardboard frame usually 2 x 2 inches in size. This transparency is a kind of undeveloped film which, looked at in the normal way, will not show a picture. But hold it up to the light from a window and the images appear. Even better, mount it on one of the machines which throws a really strong light behind the film and magnifies it at the same time. You can see exactly what you have as a picture. You can also see any bad places which will show up in the developed picture. Watch for a muddy place in the color or bubble-like spots. The color should appear clear and "transparent" and have a certain evenness.

Most people when shooting color photographs do not really know what they are doing unless they have studied the subject and have had a lot of experience. What they are really doing is painting with light the object desired in the picture. It will occur to you right away that this "art" requires more skill, time, and energy than black and white photography. So, of course, one transparency will cost you several times what a black and white print will. On a small budget perhaps only a cover will be printed in color, or one or two inside pictures combined with flat color, which is only a colored instead of black ink. The impact of color is so strong that "less is more." More about this subject in the chapter on layout.

❖ ART WORK

Even if your book relies on photographs for its illustrations, you may find some simple types of art work useful. Let us consider some of them.

Standing departments, such as the editorial, the guest column, letters to the editor, reports or news from local units, often need something to give them visual interest. Photographs are likely to be undesirable or impractical for this purpose. On the other hand, an artist can draw a suitable heading for a department which would be standing make-up for a period of time. Department headings should be clear, neat, and drawn in a modern style. They should relate to the title or content of the department, and, while they should attract attention, they should not be obtrusive. You should not try to have the title hand lettered, since most artists are not competent in lettering and also because it is an old-fashioned practice except for a special kind of display make-up. Instead, set the title in a suitable type face of the size you will use, and obtain a reproduction proof for the artist. He will include the type matter in his design.

If the department covers one or more pages, as may be true of reports from local units, decorative pieces would relieve the columns of text. For example, an artist might draw sharp black and white line sketches, thumbnail size and in a semi-cartoon style, to illustrate some of the items. This is a much more interesting device than having photos of local activities. Usually such pictures will be technically below par, and in most cases their subject matter will appeal only to the people in the photos.

If a local activity is of more than routine interest and will have a wide general appeal, it should be featured as a special story in the magazine. The editor tries to learn about such events in advance so as to arrange story and picture coverage.

Miscellaneous spots, if cleverly drawn, are good fillers for pages without other visual accent. In content, they may relate to the magazine's special field, to the time of year, to some concern of the readers. They should be simple and uncomplicated in style, perhaps just a suggestion of a picture instead of a fully plotted one. They should never be large enough to be taken for an illustration of a story. Sometimes they may be used as tailpieces, but other positions on the page are just as effective.

Some types of articles may be well illustrated with pen and ink sketches: the amusing personal experience account, an interpretative piece, the expository article for which photos are impractical. Several of the specific suggestions for content in Chapter 2 would be nicely supported by drawings of this kind. Consider the piece on the new employee, the one on "My Worst Glorious Fourth," suggestions for local program planners, an article on how to buy a car. For example, the last could be developed as straight advice or it could be witty and slightly satirical, with sketches appropriate in either case. The style of the drawings should always be consistent with the tone and content of the text. It is better to use several spot drawings in all of these examples than a single large one. Here the art is adding to the over-all impression, illuminating the main point; it is not supplying more information or providing dramatic impact.

Sometimes you may use what are called display pieces, that is, art work whose sole purpose is to make a feature look dressy. Display pieces can easily get out of hand and make a magazine look overdressed; therefore use them sparingly. Cases where they would be appropriate are: a first announcement or statement or message by the national president of an organization about a significant event, policy, or program; an unusual guest editorial; a piece, possibly an informal essay, celebrating an anniversary in which the readers are involved.

Notice the special-occasion character of these features. The kind of art work used would depend upon the purpose and content of the feature. The tone might be light and gay, or formal and dignified; the content might be illustrative or decorative; the medium might be pen and ink or brush. If your book uses color, here is a place where it may add materially to the display effect.

An editor works with an artist as he does with an author. He sends the artist a copy of the manuscript, along with the following specifications: the page size and column measure of the magazine, the kind of paper the magazine is printed on, a description of the general type of illustration desired, any special problems of reproduction that may be encountered, the way in which color may or may not be used, the deadline. He also indicates the fee. In addition, he should send sample copies of the publication if the artist is not already familiar with it. These same specifications apply also to assignments of other types of art work, including the pen and ink sketches described above. In order to make suitable and pointed drawings, the artist must thoroughly understand the text he is illustrating, its purpose, content, and function in the book. He will bring to it a fresh point of view and a distinctive imagination, so that often his illustrations communicate as happily as the text. At times, good illustrations redeem a second- or third-rate script.

❖ SOURCES OF ART

You will find it convenient to discover as many local sources of art as you can. Usually the illustrations for an issue must be made after the manuscript copy is in hand, which may mean that the time in which the artist has to work is very limited, since the printer's deadline may be approaching rapidly. Therefore, if you can turn to artists close by, you are at an advantage. You are at a further advantage if you have the services of a full-time or part-time artist. When a magazine is substantial enough to need a second person at the editorial (not secretarial) level, it is practical to employ someone who can make layouts, do some of the drawings, and handle most of the tasks involving production. He should be able to draw many of the sketches referred to above. Being thoroughly at home with the magazine's slant and editorial requirements, he can give real character to these simple illustrations. It is quite possible to arrange to have a part-time assistant if the art and production work is not too extensive.

Even when you have a staff artist or art editor, you will want some of the illustrations made outside the office in order to vary style. Often all the art work for a nonconsumer magazine will be obtained from free-lance artists. You may find free-lance artists in your community, especially if it is a large city. Artists tend to congregate in publishing centers, where their markets are. In your community they may have a professional organization through which you can get in touch with individuals. Also you may find the art editor of a local publishing house or advertising agency helpful; he may either do work himself or be able to recommend artists. The faculty of the art department of an adjacent college may be another source. Outside your locality, you can find names of likely artists from their work in books and other periodicals, although you should remember that the fees of an artist appearing in a mass-circulation commercial magazine are likely to be beyond your budget. When you have located one or more illustrators of real competence, you should try to give them assignments on a more or less regular basis. Then they would allow time for your work in their schedules and not be loaded up when you need them.

Artists vary widely both in style and type of illustration they can do well. You should maintain contact with artists whose work is of different kinds. Examine samples of their drawings carefully to see whether their work is appropriate for your book and for a particular assignment you have in mind and whether they show professional quality. Amateur art in a magazine discourages readers almost more than any other thing. They may not know just what the trouble is, but they feel something is wrong. Do not be tempted to settle for illustrations that are badly drawn, ineptly conceived, lacking in style and imagination. It is better not to have any art in your magazine than to use art which is second-rate.

Fees to artists are not standardized. Practically every artist is a free lance, and his fees are usually in direct proportion to the demand for his work. Nonconsumer magazines are not competing for the high-priced services of artists whose work appears in the editorial or advertising pages of consumer magazines. There are many good artists who are not in that class.

The editor should arrange a scale of payment according to the amount of work an art assignment requires, taking into account the time allowed the artist. The fee is higher when the deadline is close. Fees for pen and ink sketches range all the way from $15 to $25 to $35 each; and for full-dress drawings from $75 up. Keep in mind that as of this writing inflation is rampant and the fees just quoted may not be sufficient.

CHAPTER FOUR

PROCESSING THE MANUSCRIPTS

We have now reached that place in the editorial process when work on a single issue begins. Up to this point the steps have been those that are basic to all issues and frequently concern several issues at one time. When soliciting and accepting manuscripts and pictures, the editor frequently does not earmark them for a definite date. Now, however, we are ready to consider the jobs required on a given issue of the magazine before it is ready to be sent to the printer.

These jobs include selecting the specific features for an issue, processing the manuscripts, laying out the pages, and processing the pictures. All these tasks are related. In the editorial operation it is impossible to separate them entirely and to place them in any firm chronological order. For the purposes of description, however, it is possible to discuss processing the manuscripts separately as it is a more or less self-contained operation. The other three tasks are so closely bound together that they are grouped together in the next chapter. Accordingly this chapter deals with copyreading, type-styling, copy-fitting—the three steps in processing a manuscript. Before we deal with each step in detail, we must consider some preliminary matters.

The work of processing a manuscript is mainly the same for any type of printing process. Any differences may be suggested by your printer.

All your manuscripts, or final copy, now should be in good condition. Every one should be typewritten, double-spaced, with one-and-a-half-inch margins, on paper that will not smudge and is heavy enough to stand up under pencil markings and some erasures. Onionskin or rough-finish paper is not practical. Only one side of the sheet should be used. The first line of the first page of the manuscript should be dropped about three inches from the top to allow space for several kinds of marks, to be described later. Most professional writers will prepare their manuscripts in this way, but if a writer has not done so, his manuscript should be retyped in the editorial office.

By this time a manuscript should have already undergone any necessary revision or rewriting. Generally speaking, it is the author's job to revise a manuscript, if necessary, which he does under the editor's supervision, as explained in Chapter 3. Rewriting, on the other hand, is done by the editor and is an entirely different process. To rewrite means to make a readable story out of facts that have already been assembled. For instance, the editor of a house publication will probably rewrite many of the reports sent in by the departments of the organization. Or the news reports from local units of an organization will be rewritten by the editor of the national journal. Often the editor brings more journalistic skill to this job than the local reporters; he can make the story a suitable length; and he may want to work up these reports in a consistent style. What he needs from the reporters are the facts, including the names of people, correctly spelled.

In any case, all the manuscripts are now in their complete and final form as far as content is concerned. Even so, a considerable amount of editorial work remains to be done in preparing them for printing. This is the time when the editor takes in hand his "blue pencil," a term that has become an editor's trademark because he often does use a blue pencil in processing manuscripts and proof. Pencils are one of the editor's tools. Every editor should supply himself with several kinds, carefully selected. You will need black and several colors. The lead should be hard enough so that the lines do not quickly become thick and make the writing illegible, but not so hard as to be brittle and therefore to break easily under pressure. It is a good idea to test out various brands to see which ones work best for you. At the same time, you should test colors to find those that function best. The reasons for using colored pencils is that on every manuscript, dummy sheet, and page of proof you must make marks for several different purposes. If you consistently use the same color for the same kind, the printer and others who must be guided by those marks can more easily understand your instructions and so reduce the number of mistakes.

As you will see in the sections below, copyreading, type-styling, and fitting involve marking manuscripts in special ways. For each of these purposes you might well use a different colored pencil. Black is good for copyreading because it erases easily and is readily identified as part of the copy.

Type-styling indications, on the other hand, are not a part of the copy but directions to the printer. Therefore a color is advisable, to distinguish them clearly from the copy. The color should be strong and clear; brown, purple, and blue are possibilities whereas green is not practical because even a dark shade tends not to show up well on white paper. Select another color for fitting, especially for cutting a manuscript after it has been measured for length; this color makes it easy to identify this cutting from cutting done prior to the fitting stage. You can thus facilitate your calculations as well as make it possible to check these calculations later. You may find red a good color for fitting, but beware of the shade— blue-red, not orange-red, is advisable, since even a small amount of marking in red will vibrate and add to the difficulty of reading. Also, red in any shade does not erase well. Never use a red pencil for writing words; lines drawn through copy to indicate a cut after measurement is probably the only good use for a red pencil.

You also need at least two reference books which you will use continually in copyreading, a dictionary and a style manual. For a dictionary, you cannot do better than *Webster's New International Dictionary* (published by G. and C. Merriam Company), probably the third edition. The abridged edition for desk use is adequate, although a sizable editorial establishment should have the unabridged edition. Be sure that the edition you use is current.

Some editors prefer the second edition (these books are sometimes referred to in editorial offices as W-2 and W-3) but the desk edition is already out of print so that is impractical. There are some good new dictionaries. Examine *The*

American Heritage Dictionary of the English Language (Houghton Mifflin Co.). The book is rather large for desk use but useful all the same. Other types of dictionaries of interest to copyreaders are discussed in "The Editor's Bookshelf," the bibliographical note to this book.

A manual of style sets a standard for practices of capitalization, punctuation, syntax, the use of quotation marks, italics, and the like. Every magazine needs an established style in matters of this kind in order to be consistent. Following this style will avoid such inconsistencies as having "co-operate" on one page and "cooperate" on another, or "colour" and "color," or "Church and state" and "church and state."

The University of Chicago Press's *A Manual of Style* is widely used. (The titles of other stylebooks appear in "The Editor's Bookshelf.") To this manual you may want to add some well-defined practices of style that are peculiar to your field.

❧ COPYREADING

Copyreading is sometimes called editing, but it should not be assumed from the latter term that this task is the editor's sole responsibility respecting a manuscript. In the preceding chapters we have explored the various tasks an editor performs in connection with manuscripts before they are ready to be copyread. The editor of a substantial magazine may not do any copyreading, but rather delegate that job to someone who is likely to be even more expert than he is. With most small magazines, however, the editor is likely to be responsible for copyreading the manuscripts. He should, therefore, make himself as proficient as possible, for copyreading is a fine skill. To copyread means to make the manuscript grammatical, that is, to bring it in line with good English usage; to make it stylistically consistent; and, by making minor modifications, to enhance its readability. Let us consider each of these functions in turn.

ENGLISH USAGE. In the English language, there are no absolute rules of grammar, only practices of good usage which are collated and standardized by recognized experts who produce grammars, dictionaries, and stylebooks. Therefore, the aim of the copyreader is for reasonable, not absolute, correctness. He understands that English as a living language is continually changing. A construction that was "bad" in grandfather's day may be permitted today and become "good" tomorrow. A case in point is the practice of not ending a sentence with a preposition. Today, only the real purists among grammarians insist on following that practice absolutely. Avoiding a preposition at the end of a sentence often causes it to be prim and stilted. A pertinent old chestnut is credited to Winston Churchill. When he was confronted with the rule, he wanted to know if he would be supposed to say: "That is something up with which I will not put." Many semicolloquial but very communicative verbs include prepositions. *Put up with* is, of course, one of them. "That is something I will not put up with" is a stronger sentence than its "grammatical" equivalent, "I will not put up with that."

Another example of change in usage concerns the split infinitive, that is, the infinitive with a word, usually an adverb, inserted between "to" and the rest of the verb. Split infinitives that are awkward and unnecessary should be avoided. However, should transferring the word or words splitting an infinitive cause a sentence to be stilted or ambiguous, that sentence should either be left as is or recast. There are various other points about which the copyreader must be attentive, for example, confusing sequence of tenses; lack of agreement in number between subject and verb; too frequently used pronouns whose antecedents are not well established. These require a vigilant eye.

The primary purpose of the copyreader in making a manuscript grammatical is to clarify meaning, not to make the language reach a given standard of grammatical "purity." Therefore, effectiveness of communication is more important than considerations of grammar. Some authors employ a style that is colloquial to the point of infringing on good usage, although there is never doubt as to meaning. For a copyreader to try to "clean up" a manuscript of such an author is a violation of the author's intent and his integrity as an artist. Other writers use a truncated or staccato style that does not conform to the conventions of sentence structure. Here again the copyreader does not interfere or tamper with the author's basic literary style.

CONSISTENT STYLE. As was noted above, this function of copyreading concerns such questions as spelling, punctuation, and the use of hyphens, quotation marks, and italics. Every manuscript will require some corrections of this kind. Probably no author scrutinizes his manuscript with the same care as a copyreader does, because the author's main interest is content. And some authors, even those who turn in highly acceptable copy, are weak in spelling and the fine points of

English usage. It is the copyreader's job to be proficient in these matters. Do not be too hesitant or too lazy to look up moot points or those you do not know. In fact, if you study your stylebook, your eye will become more alert to things in manuscripts that should be corrected.

READABILITY. This function does not refer to the over-all readability of the manuscript; it should be assumed that judgment on this point was made when the manuscript was accepted. The copyreader checks certain details to see whether minor modification would bring about improvement in communication. The details which should be checked are: the first sentence or paragraph, to see that the lead is a good one; the conclusion, to see that the piece adds up well; paragraphing and sentence structure thoughout the manuscript.

Because the life of a magazine is very short, it is vital that each feature have a lead, or first paragraph, which draws the reader's attention to it immediately. Therefore, you should ask, "Is this lead going to make a person want to read the rest of the article?" There may be a simple way in which you can improve the lead. For example, you may want to reorder the first sentence to make it direct, instead of indirect, or to make two sentences out of a long, complicated one, or to substitute a specific, even provocative, word for a vague one.

On the optimistic assumption that the reader is going to get to the end, make sure the article comes to a real stop and does not leave the reader dangling. It is even permissible to write a concluding sentence provided it is in full harmony with the author's thought. If the author's last paragraph sounds like an afterthought, perhaps it should be transferred to an earlier spot; another paragraph may serve better as a conclusion.

As you copyread a manuscript, observe the paragraphing. Paragraphs suggest the framework of the article and help the reader to grasp the progression of ideas or the flow of information. Trained journalists have learned to write in short paragraphs; and even though some of them overdo it, it is still a good idea. Break up long paragraphs in your manuscripts unless doing so would interfere with the author's intention. An occasional long paragraph may serve a special purpose.

Also watch for overly involved sentences. Simply inserting a period and a subject to make two sentences out of one will sometimes enhance readability without cramping or changing the writer's style. Some writers, even good ones, are addicted to the "There is" and "There are" construction. Forms of the verb "to be" are usually weak in a sentence. Such sentences may be reconstructed so as to bring forward a stronger verb.

Part of the copyreader's job is to check quotations in manuscripts for accuracy and to make sure that no infringement of copyright will be involved in printing them (a subject which is covered in detail in Chapter 7). In reading and marking both copy and proof, the editor uses a number of standard copyreader's marks, a kind of shorthand understood by editors and printers alike. You should become familiar with them as quickly as you can. Facsimile pages showing edited copy appear in most stylebooks and in many dictionaries.

In all copyreading, you should be sure that you do not in any way change the content of the story or modify the author's ideas or style. Such changes constitute revision which, as was said above, is the author's responsibility. The only exceptions would be when the editor had asked the author's permission to make certain carefully specified revisions, or when the author had requested that such revisions be made in the editorial office. The temptation of the neophyte is to make too many changes in copy. Use your pencil sparingly and have sound reasons for every mark you make.

❧ TYPE-STYLING

Every magazine should have an established typographic design, that is, each element—the text, subheads, blurbs, and captions—will be set in a particular size and style whenever it appears. At the time copy for a given issue is prepared for the printer, major decisions on typography have already been made. The type faces have been chosen and the sizes and styles for the various elements decided on. Even so, the manuscripts of each issue must be marked in detail to conform with this design. Such marks constitute part of the essential directions to the printer.

If any feature has more than one page of copy, it is necessary to indicate the type-styling on the first page only. The specifications for the text are usually placed in the upper left-hand margin. They include type face, type size, and the size of the slug on which it is to be set, as well as the column measure. For instance, a manuscript might carry this notation: "9/10 Bodoni Book, 15 picas." On the first page, specify also the headline type, which should be indicated again on the dummy, since it is improbable that the same operator will set both the body of the magazine and the heads, captions, and other incidentals. For the same reason, copy for captions and blurbs should be typed on separate sheets, and appropriate typographical directions should be given on each.

If your book is large enough to carry stories of considerable length, some method of visually breaking up the text is usually desirable. Full columns of solid type look formidable to most readers.

If your page is anywhere from 36 to 72 picas or more in depth, you may break the columns by inserting white space at appropriate places. Such spaces may be from 1 to 3 picas deep, depending on the depth of the page. Some editors like to use an initial letter to begin a section which follows space. An initial (a large capital of a face related to the body type) may be either ascending or descending, that is, it may "stick up" above the first line of type or "sink" to align with the base of the second or third line in the paragraph. In either case, an initial should not attract undue attention to itself, for its purpose is to facilitate, not to impede, reading. An initial, when used, is most often found only at the beginning of a piece.

This conventional way of breaking up the page is still used but is considered old-fashioned. On a fairly large page a short interesting quote from the article may be printed in a large size type with cut off rules top and bottom. When initials are used in such quotes they are nearly always in a dramatic type design very different from the body.

Setting in small capitals a word or two of the first line of copy after a break is also a common practice. (Small capitals are of the same height as lower case letters.) Some typographers frown on small capitals used in this way, and probably they should not be so used except for very special purposes. However, if a large page has no element of visual interest, this treatment of the column break may be justified.

Another way to break up columns of solid text is to insert subheads at suitable places. This practice is recommended only when a piece is quite long and when the subheads will help the reader to follow the development of the subject. In other words, subheads should enhance the meaning and import of the copy; they should not be used simply as visual accents. Good subheads assist the reader to grasp the organization of the article and to follow the continuity of ideas. For that reason, they may be effectively employed in long passages of exposition and analysis, and, in fact, may constitute an outline of the content. Such copy may or may not have a place in your small magazine. If you use subheads, keep them as short as possible; if they extend to a full line or more, they give a scrappy and unattractive appearance. Extreme variation in the length of subheads is also hard to handle. In any case, the type face of the subhead should conform to the body type. Bold face caps and lower case would be a good selection, as would small caps of the text size.

If your page carries two or more columns, the breaks, however they are styled, should not fall opposite one another, because this would produce an awkward band of horizontal white space. Nor should a break occur less than seven lines from the top or bottom of the page. This means that the copyreader must provide these breaks not only in relation to the content of the story, but also in relation to their predicted place on the page. He, therefore, does not mark them on the copy until after the layout is made. He must indicate the exact amount of space to be inserted and specify type for subheads. The amount of space for breaks must be consistent throughout the copy. This job is really a part of fitting, which is discussed in the next section of this chapter.

Visual breaks are usually not needed when the article is illustrated with several pictures.

Although you work within a basic design, you will have one or more features in each issue that should receive special typographic treatment. The over-all plan for the book's appearance will establish its personality and character, so that the reader, knowing what to expect, is not shocked by the total unfamiliarity of each issue. The familiar has recognized public appeal. On the other hand, if the appearance of the magazine gives the impression of always being exactly the same, before long the reader will find it monotonous. Therefore, use your inventiveness in working up something for each issue that is deliberately a variation or a break in your basic design. In addition to the display features described in other chapters, you may also use one or more spot features for this change of pace. However, when these spot features appear too frequently, they tend to cancel the dramatic element of one another. Features that are suitable for spot treatment are announcements of various kinds, anything of brief compass which you want to call to your readers' attention; short, appropriate statements from people of particular interest to your constituency, the president of the company, the executive secretary of the organization, committee members; highlights of your next issue; special news bulletins.

Display in such features may be attained by using a head that is set in a face different from the regular one, by a change in the column measure, by a type for the text different from the usual body type, by a smart use of type rules, by blocks or free-form masses of color. Remember, however, that all these elements are like whipped cream: it is easy to get too much of them. Restraint and simplicity are the two watchwords in the use of display, but they are achieved usually through hard experience. The beginning editor is inclined to be too fussy and to want to use every device at once. Another watchword is suitability. Although you are working for a clear break in your design, you do not want the spots to have a foreign appearance, as if they did not belong in the family. They should be striking and dramatic, but not startling, shocking, or inappropriate. Depend upon your good taste, a sharp eye, and experience to teach you your way around.

Let us take a few examples. If your page has three columns, a display feature might be set in a line slightly narrower than the width of two columns. This would allow for a pleasing indention. But because the line is longer, you should go to a type size that is larger than that of the regular body type. The text should be long enough to obtain a good proportion between the width and depth of the display matter. If the two-column feature is shorter than page length, use an attractive cut-off rule so that it will not fuse with regular text. The title for the feature might be set in a smaller size type than regular heads. Consider placing the title flush to the left margin and the text flush to the right. The by-line could probably be set in regular style, or it might be placed at the end in a way to fill out the last line, or else it might be set below the last line, flush on the right.

For a shorter feature, something quick and splashy— maybe the announcement of the place and date of your national convention—select a one-word head and set it in a face that is really bold yet blends with your over-all design. Your printer will have some of these display letters, generally for advertisements, which, if used sparingly, will add interest to your page. If your body type is a modern face, such as Bodoni, your one-word title might be set in a gothic, or sans serif, letter and the brief text in a similar face in lines of uneven length. Consider the title in color, or a vertical rectangular block flush to the left with the lines uneven on the right, or a couple of arrows at strategic spots.

In any case, the editor must work out such matters in detail and mark his copy and his dummy pages to conform with his plan. This is done in cooperation with the person who makes the layouts, if the editor does not make them himself. It is possible, too, for an inexperienced editor to get some help from his printer.

❧ FITTING

One of the major steps in processing copy for a magazine is arranging the lines of type and the illustrations so that each page is neatly filled. In other words, the copy in a periodical must "fit," as the jargon of the trade expresses it. In a book, various techniques can be used for compressing or stretching copy to fill a certain number of pages, but the number of pages is not always fixed and certain pages may carry only a few lines. There may even be "blanks." In a magazine, on the other hand, every page is filled and the amount of copy of each issue is determined by a fixed number of pages. Perhaps you have wondered how it happens that an article ends neatly at the bottom of the page, or with just enough space left for that brief, amusing anecdote. Of course it does not just happen! The editor has maneuvered skillfully to make it come out that way to avoid a makeshift or patched appearance. The task involved is called "fitting."

A rough estimate of the length of a manuscript can be made by a word count. A double-spaced typewritten page with normal margins will carry between 300 and 350 words in elite type, and between 275 and 325 words in pica type. Another gauge is that eight normal lines of typewritten text in elite type or ten lines in pica type will run to about 100 words. "Elite" refers to the small and "pica" to the large type-writer type.

Some of the new typewriters have type faces which resemble printing types and, like printing types, have "proportional spacing." On these machines every letter does not occupy the same amount of horizontal space, the wider letters requiring more space than the narrow ones. These machines are being used more and more. If a manuscript comes to you typed on one of them, you must calculate the average number of characters per inch or per line.

The number of words in a manuscript will give you a measure that is accurate enough to enable you to decide whether or not it is of suitable length for your general purposes, but it is at best only a rough estimate. What you must know when processing the manuscript for printing is how much space in the book it will require, that is, the exact number of lines of printed type the script will make.

The way to obtain this figure is to convert lines of typewritten text into lines of printed text. To make this conversion, that is, to estimate the number of type lines any manuscript will make, you must actually count the number of characters (letters) it contains, including the spaces between words. This is not as tedious as you might suppose. Find the right-hand end of the shortest full line on the typed page. At that point draw a vertical line, up and down, parallel to the right edge of the page. Count the number of characters in this shortest line. Suppose this number is 72. You will, of course, have lines with a few characters over.

For the next step, you must know the number of characters in a line of type as printed in your magazine. For the present example, we shall say that this number is 48. Say that in a certain paragraph you have 7 full lines. Not counting the characters which hang to the right of the vertical line, these 7 full lines will make 11 type lines, an answer easily arrived at because one line of 72 characters is quickly calculated as making a line and a half of type (the half line at the end of a paragraph must, of course, be counted as a full line). Say now that you have 30 characters over these 7 lines of 72s. These 30 characters will fill the half line of type and run over on another line. Your final figure for the first paragraph, therefore, is 12. Note it lightly on the right margin at the end of the paragraph and proceed in the same way with each paragraph. The sum of the figures for each paragraph is a reliable estimate of the number of type lines your manuscript will occupy. With a little practice you will learn further short cuts.

Now it is necessary to find out how we got the figure 48. This number is based upon the length of the line and the kind and size of type face used, all of which are a part of the specifications of the typography for your magazine. The specifications also include the exact measurements (width and depth) of the column and the page. Page as used here is the type page and does not include margins. To understand these measurements you must know the term "pica," which is the standard unit of measurement in typography, which has nothing to do with the typewriter. The pica is equal to 12 points or one-sixth of an inch. Therefore six picas equal one inch. Let us now take an example of specifications for the typography of a small magazine. They might be as follows:

Type face: De Vinne

Type size: 10 point on 11-point slug (abbreviated "10/11 pt"); this means that there will be one point of space between lines

Column measure (that is, the width of the column): 19 picas

Depth of column: 62 lines (about 57 picas)

Type faces differ in design and, therefore, different faces of the same size will not have the same number of characters per pica. De Vinne set in 10 point averages about 2.5 characters per pica. There will be, therefore, 48 characters per line. Your printer will supply you with a set of character count tables that give the number of characters per pica for the various type faces in their different sizes available in his shop. Some editors find it convenient to have all manuscripts typed in lines containing the number of characters of the printed line. In the example given above the typewriter margins would be set for lines of 48 characters. The right-hand margin would be uneven, of course, but even so a fairly fast calculation is possible by this method.

You are now prepared to estimate the length of a manuscript in type lines. You must have this line count for each manuscript as you make the layouts for an issue of your publication.

Another way of finding out the length of a manuscript is to have the printer set it up in type and provide a galley proof. This galley proof is a continuous column of type printed on a long sheet of paper. The type matter has not been divided into pages at this point. By simply measuring with a ruler, you can know quickly the number of lines. And by cutting the galleys into column lengths and laying them on a page of the magazine, you can see where the type matter will fall. When making a layout, you can pin or paste parts of the galley to the dummy sheet and so allocate the exact number of lines you wish at any position on the page.

The drawback in using galleys is that it is expensive and takes time. If you find you want to cut the amount of copy, you must then pay the printer for type composition you will not use, and unless you cut whole paragraphs, you will pay dearly for all resetting of parts in which you have made changes. Even if you make no alterations in the galleys, the printer will charge for supplying these proofs.

Most small magazines can get along very well without galleys by making careful and detailed layouts and by accurately estimating type lines. The first proof you receive from the printer will be a page proof, which will show the text and pictures made up into pages according to the dummy you have supplied with your copy. Whether or not you decide to work from a galley will depend upon your particular situation.

It is likely that your book will have the same number of pages in each issue. The variation in the number of pages in a commercial magazine is caused by the amount of space needed for advertisements. Each week, or month, or quarter, you must have sufficient copy to fit exactly the four, eight, sixteen, or however many pages your magazine contains. A rule of thumb is that the fewer pages you have, the easier it is to fill them but the harder it is to fit the copy to the space. Therefore, you learn various ways to trim and to pad a feature to make it fit into a prescribed amount of space.

Unless it is very expertly or compactly written, any manuscript can withstand some judicious pruning. To cut a considerable number of lines, first consider limiting the subject matter and deleting an entire section of several paragraphs that will not weaken the manuscript as a whole. Failing that, see what sentences may go from each section, but be careful to preserve continuity and flow. Do not cut the "color," that is, the descriptive and specific details, for although they may seem secondary, they give the lift to writing. It is better to run your pencil through the generalizations and vague statements. The writing of nonprofessionals can frequently be trimmed at the beginning and the end, for the skill of knowing when to start and when to stop is painfully acquired only after much practice. Any of these cuts must be consistent with the principles of editing and with the policy governing the changing of an author's work described earlier in this chapter.

These suggestions for making a manuscript shorter apply to any writing the editor does himself. In fact it is possible, and considered quite professional in the magazine world, to write to space. Suppose you are writing for a house organ a piece on unusual vacations some of the employees have taken. You have enough material plus some photographs for an attractive two-page spread. You may even make the layout before you write the article, deciding at that time the number of lines of copy appropriate to the subject of your article and, also, to the space for text in your layout. You select and organize the content of your article within that limit. Of course, if the number of lines seems impractical after you see the words on paper, some adjustment must be made. With practice you can learn, however, to make reasonable predictions as to the line count of articles you will write.

Making a manuscript longer does not mean adding paragraphs unless the author is asked to do it. It means adjusting the layout so that the type lines and the illustrations will fit the allotted space. An editorial note, or blurb, may be added to the copy and placed in such a way on the page to take up a required number of lines. If, for example, the vacation piece fell ten lines short, it is easy to fill the space with a blurb, which would not necessarily come to ten lines.

The principle to keep in mind in fitting your copy is that the pages must look planned and orderly to the reader. He must not get the impression that something has been added just to take up space, or that the book has been thrown together in a haphazard way. To prevent that impression takes editorial thought and care.

Several last-minute editorial chores remain in this process of preparing copy. Just before sending the book to the printer, remove all staples, clips, or anything else holding the pages together; assemble the pages in the order of their place in the book; mark each page of manuscript or feature to show the name and issue of the magazine and the corresponding number of the page in the magazine. For example: *Weight Watchers Magazine,* February 1976, pages 3 and 4. Then number the pages of the assembled manuscripts consecutively from front to back. These marks might well go in color at the upper right-hand margin.

Type a list of the contents showing exact titles, by-lines, and page numbers. If your book is large enough to include a table of contents, copy for this page will suffice for this list. It is all right to attach to this copy a tear sheet of the contents page of the latest issue in print and mark on it, "follow style." The same is true of copy for the postal notice and for the imprint, which is the arrangement for identifying the publisher and editorial staff, and the volume and number if they are a part of your book.

Your manuscript copy is now processed and ready for typesetting. But before the complete issue can be sent to the printer, layouts must be made and the illustrations processed. We turn to that topic in the next chapter.

This entire description has assumed letterpress printing. The additional tasks in processing manuscripts for some kinds of offset printing will be described in Chapter 6, "Printing the Magazine."

CHAPTER FIVE

HINTS ON LAYOUT

In the sequence of building your magazine, you have now come to the point where you must decide how this particular issue will look and its general impression on the reader. This chapter deals with matters so close to the chapter on printing that they should hardly be separated, and yet I believe understanding will be clearer if we treat them separately, pointing out relationships. This will mean a few unavoidable repetitions.

WHAT TO THINK ABOUT IN ADVANCE

Basic to making up a single issue is the kind of printing process to be used. Will it be printed by letterpresss? If so, you have probably already decided on the type face for the body of the text and for headlines, captions, blurbs, and the like. And your copy has been so marked. (See Chapter 4, "Processing the Manuscripts.") Also, your magazine is probably quite substantial.

If you use one of the minipress operations or an inexpensive offset process using photography to print the book, what you will do about your copy and pictures will be quite different. We think the latter is likely to be the case because it allows you to produce your magazine much more cheaply, and has the advantage, which will sometimes be desirable, of a lighter and more informal over-all appearance. If more dignity in appearance is desirable, that is possible, also. That difference is one of the decisions you make as you lay out the pages. So let us say some specific things about layout.

❖ HOW TO START

The kinds of layout of even one issue should be consistent with the general design of the magazine—formal and dignified, flashy and entertaining, deliberately *avant-garde*. This decision will be made when all the first thinking about the magazine is finished. More on this subject appears in Chapter 9. In any case, the design, and hence the layouts, are expected to appeal to the kind of reader you want to attract, just as much as the content. Whether or not to make a layout that is inventive and outside your usual style is whether or not you think your readers will be unpleasantly startled or glad to see something "different."

Some simple tools are essential to laying out your pages: a pica ruler made of metal that will permit you to establish a square edge, a plastic triangle that will give you a true right angle and help in drawing straight lines quickly. Some rubber cement that allows you to paste pieces down but also pull them off again easily. Rubber cement gets very thick with age, so get some thinner at the same time. Also lots of pencils of different kinds—grease pencils and even crayons, some in color, some with thick and others with thin lines. As we proceed you will see how to use these tools.

Your printer should supply you with "dummy sheets." They are sheets of paper that are marked off with rules to show you the printed area of the page.

We assume you have already decided on the content and have the copy in good shape. And you have the photos and/or art work in hand. You are ready for paging, deciding which features go where on the pages. Take into account the length of each one, its importance or weight in the book, and the impression on the reader as he turns the pages.

The first feature is a crucial item whether or not you have a self cover or a detached cover. For this example we are assuming two-columns on the page. If the page is sizable (e.g., 8 x 12 or 10), more than one feature can begin the issue, especially if your policy is to have short pieces. On the other hand a well selected picture or two with a single article may be more likely to get the reader going.

And here we are at the critical subject of what you do about pictures. Placement and size are not only essential, they go together. The photograph in your hand may be 8 x 10 inches, obviously too big. Nearly all prints are reduced in size for reproduction because it makes the images sharper, or the diffused images less fuzzy. Remember what was said earlier about "low definition." Pictures are reduced proportionately, of course. One-half width will produce one-half depth unless you manage some judicious cropping. More on cropping a little later.

Whether or not the picture will be reproduced by offset or letterpress, you give the printer very specific instructions on size of pictures. Here is how. Suppose you want your main photo almost the full width of the page, say 24 picas. In that case you want to establish how deep it will be at that width. Take a ruler, or plastic triangle, or heavy piece of paper, anything that will not slide easily, and place it diagonally from the upper left to bottom right corners of the picture. Then place your pica ruler at a right angle at the bottom of the print and move it up until 24 picas intercepts the diagonal. The depth of the reduced print will be the distance from the intersection to the top of the print. The diagonal must never be drawn, even on the reverse side of the photo. If that is a suitable depth you have established the dimensions of the print as reduced.

Using a dummy sheet, decide where on the page this picture will be placed in relation to text, title and any other pictures, and draw an accurate outline in that position being sure to use a ruler that will make a square edge, your triangle or pica ruler. On the reverse side of the photo mark very lightly "24 picas wide" as your instructions to the printer. This process is the same with every picture in your book. If you have a pen and ink sketch with no square edges, mark them off with a ruler and proceed as before. This sketch when reproduced will seem smaller than it is because of the surrounding white space.

If you have a second picture for this first page, you might make it a little more than half the width of the other picture (say, 18 or 20 picas) and place it flush against the larger picture at the right hand lower margin. You now have some space between the two pictures on the left hand side. It might be used for the title, some words about the pictures which substitute for captions, and even the first sentence of the piece which continues on to the bottom of the right hand column. If the piece ends there, leave a 3-pica space for the by-line. The photo credit, if necessary might be placed between the two pictures. Use a type smaller than the body type. You might treat the by-line this way even if the text continues to the next page.

It is important to find out whether or not the type beginning with the title will go easily and nicely into this space. So count the spaces of the title, knowing the size of type, to see how long it is—how many picas does it measure? If it is too long, it must turn over, making two lines. You measure the space needed by using your pica ruler. Leave one pica below the big picture and one at the side of the samll one. If the space is too small, use a different title or change the layout. If the title is short, center it in the space and the surrounding white space will look quite neat. In any case draw lines showing the exact size and placement of the title.

❖ DIFFERING STYLES

What you have now is a fair example of a contemporary, and conservative, layout style. What are your readers like? Are they ladies who belong to a fairly large club such as a state or regional garden club? If so, this style would be okay. But if your magazine circulates to a club of motorcyclists, it would not do. (These examples are selected because of their very different types of audience.) In this case the layout must have punch and the title must be pungent and probably printed quite large. Same for the main picture. Perhaps it might be a large circle if it lends itself to that form and the title printed around the circle. One fairly obvious example is the dramatic face and shoulders of a rider on his bike taken in a close shot showing only the upper front of the machine.

There is an old, well established rule that the subject must never be shot looking into the camera. It has and still does make good visual sense. But in this case it might be abandoned. The rider should be geared up, helmet and all, and he should be looking straight at the reader and grinning! It is hoped he has a nice come-on grin. This sort of thing used to make purist-type designers shudder, but no longer. And why? The reason such a "mug shot" is now acceptable is the desire of all editors to involve their readers as immediately as possible in the magazine. The reader has the illusion that the rider is looking directly at him.

The other picture would be the usual rectangle and its caption used to get the reader to turn the page. Or if there is a tie-in between the pictures, place it close to the circle in some dramatic way.

Now this is just a general look at the kind of dramatic layouts that appeal to young adult sportsmen. To the conventional designer the layout just described lacks taste and is more or less a horror. But it is mild compared to the real shockers. The first issue of the magazine *Southern Voices* (Spring '74) had a cover that seemed to some so exaggerated in color and design as to be ambiguous. One comment was: "Oh, all it's supposed to do is tell you we have really left behind the magnolias." By contrast the body text is small and crowded, and could not be more conventional in appearance. But then comes a double page color spread that is a real shocker. By that is meant its design, not its content. Can you tell from this description how the editor views his readers? It should be said that *Southern Voices* contains ads and may or may not be a "small magazine," because it proclaims serious intellectual purposes. Many consumer magazines do also.

So, let us consider the shock technique once in a while in layout, photos, and art work. Too many shockers become boring. Let us also remember taste, which applies to shockers as well as to other styles. To use bad taste or to be deliberately offensive is not appropriate to the small magazine field.

In laying out your pages, balance, variety, and surprise are serviceable qualities. Make your pages look different. If you have only a four page fold make the issues look different, but not so much so that the reader is not sure this is his familiar friend. Vary a complex page with a simple one. At some time do something quite unexpected so as to pleasantly surprise your readers.

Make each double page spread a visual unit so the several features will not compete with one another. Do not put two titles next to each other, because they cancel each other out. In general, the eye quickly scans a page by running rapidly from upper left and making a big swing diagonally downward. The reader is usually unconscious of this eye movement in observing a page but the editor should not be.

The fashion now in layouts is not to be uptight. In designing your pages this means not much balance, or equal parts, or layouts that are static and pictures that do not say much.

In photos and art, avoid the pretty, the precious, the cute. Get a lot of drama if you can. Drama is produced by eliminating meaningless objects and taking the shot as close up as will preserve the message. Have you noticed that the full figure has almost disappeared except in fashion magazines?

Suppose your organization has elected new officers. To line them up against the wall in a straight-on shot is not going to produce much interest in your readers. If you can find a suitable place, ask the photographer to arrange them informally in different bodily positions and in varied relation to one another. His problem will be to make a pleasing informal composition. Or you may ask him to take each one singly in full figure about the same distance from the camera. When you make your layout you can crop the pictures to face and shoulders, perhaps, and arrange these photos in a pleasing group on your page. Experiment with pieces of colored paper the shape and size of the photos when cropped. March them flush down the page in a vertical line, using the rest of the space in an article about them. Or use each one separately with a rather long caption, giving all the information in that way, and arrange them in a pleasing pattern. In this instance your title might be placed in the middle of the page in a small block, or horizontally across the page in one line. It should be part of the design or layout of the page.

A word about what "cropping" a photo means. The purpose is to change the shape or size or dimensions of the picture, or to eliminate unwanted features. The print itself is not changed. The printer when reproducing the picture just masks out the part to be cropped from the print. The editor gives him instructions with a light pencil on the reverse of the print using a pica ruler and being very accurate in measurements. To see how the picture will look when cropped, hold it up to the light or mask the areas to be cropped. Some film is developed on opaque paper which is undesirable if it is going to be reproduced. Speak to your photographer about that.

In the layout being described the captions should be approximately the same length, several lines, and may be placed at the side, bottom, or top of the picture. Be sure that the reader is not confused as to which picture the caption is related to. In this instance the captions may be printed in a different type face from the usual one. These suggestions apply to a group of officers from 4 to 8. If less or more than that number, a different approach is called for.

The convention that only a few typestyles should be used in a magazine and always the same ones has gone by the board. It is easy, however, to lapse into bad taste on this point, but even so, a loosening up of this convention has occurred.

To return to our illustration, one more layout may work well. If you have the right number, crop in the same way as above but make a square, by placing them flush with one another, or make another form if you are clever. The size of the square will depend on the number of pictures and size of page but it should be large enough to get attention. You place it in a position on the page that looks well with the amount of text used.

So far we have been considering several layout styles suitable for some kinds of readers, all of them in general use. But especially today we should recognize the *avant-garde* because of its influence and also because it is often amusing and edifying.

The use of newsprint or other paper with even a rougher surface is frequently used. Compared to the kind of stock we have so far assumed, this paper is sometimes quite cheap and also quite attractive. There is, or was (these small magazines go in and out of the market quickly), an attractive piece printed on very rough stock in a tow sacking color, its 16 pages assembled in an (approximately) 8 x 10 format but not stapled. The most striking element was that it was printed in black, and on every page was at least one sketch drawn with only a few sharp lines made with a brush or pencil, but saying something equally sharp. The content was mostly book reviews and occasionally a short essay on the current scene. Think how much less interesting this magazine would have been in color.

Another *avant-garde* piece was called *Unfold* and that is what it meant. The shape in which it arrived was about 3 x 9 inches. It showed the title and tag lines for the features. You began unfolding and the final size was about two newspaper pages. The features were printed any which way so that the reader had to turn it round and round. The stock was colored, and other colors were used flat on the inside. When you think of printing a variety of color on colored stock the number of colors you come up with may be startling or even nauseating. The content consisted of items of current interest on the arts, and the sponsoring body was a group of churches.

Let us take one more example, a small magazine in size about 8 x 12 with a substantial number of pages, with an article on world hunger. We can imagine the thinking of the editor: the pitiful Asian child with an empty rice bowl, an obviously starving family in the door of the run-down shack. All very obvious and in his mind over-used. An *avant* (an old French word meaning "before") editor is not going to be caught with anything like that. What eventually appeared was a colored picture of a red apple, with one bite out, magnified about four times. It filled the first page—a left-hand one—and the text and title were rather discreetly used on the facing right-hand page. This editor was questioned repeatedly about what the picture meant. However, some people got the idea immediately. The editor's answer was always the same, "Food," he said, "how it feels to have it and not have it."

When using color think of it as whipped cream, easy to get too much, and too much is a mark of the amateur. Also it is easy to obscure the text with color. Again, do you want your readers to read or just look at your book? Here are two ways to use flat color: to give an accent to something, or to relieve an unillustrated page by using a frame around the page in color and, if appropriate, overprinting on the frame a slogan related to the article in a repeat pattern. Be careful, though, to make this arrangement enhance and not subvert the text. Strong colors are much better than light ones except when overprinting. Avoid a lot of pastel color because it weakens the general impression. If full color is available use it sparingly and dramatically and make it say something really important, as the red apple did. In a small magazine with just a few pages, use only one transparency in each issue, sometimes on the cover and sometimes not.

❖ GETTING ALONG WITHOUT RULES

It is almost true to say there are no rules in laying out your pages, but not quite. To be completely spontaneous on an "anything goes" position usually leads to trouble. You may find yourself competing with yourself. Each issue must be more daring and startling than the last. Also you may be working with your editorial colleagues in mind instead of your readers. When each issue is almost entirely new you have so many decisions to make that your imagination runs dry, not to say your physical and psychic energy.

So some rules really are helpful in supporting innovative ideas. Let us consider a few. Suppose you decide that some things will be the same in each issue: the name of the magazine, the size and number of pages, the frequency of issue. These decisions would make your readers sure they are not reading a leaflet or brochure. One good rule would be always to ask yourself "Is this corny?"—unless corniness is the name of your game. Another question would be "Are we *too* campy or self-conscious?" To be "campy" is to cleverly spoof the past. And you see it in high and low forms. And probably the best rule of all is to remember that "avant" becomes less so every year or even every six months. Instead of "before" it becomes "behind."

The editor of the small magazine follows the trends of publishing and the times in general according to his and his readers' tastes and interests. The times right now are for the jump, the swing, the letting go, the loosening and even giving up of time-honored styles of design. We find the large mass, not the delicate decoration, the swift pace rather than the measured tread. Movement and inwardness are the words that describe much of our culture today. By inwardness we mean two things—involving your reader in your pages so he feels he is inside, and an approach to content that takes account of his human and humane existence. As just one example, "you" is a pronoun that speaks directly to a person but "one" is a pronoun that is an abstraction. Try for these qualities in your layouts including titles, pictures, and captions.

CHAPTER SIX

PRINTING THE MAGAZINE

The appearance of a magazine depends not only on how well the editor has handled the editorial process but also on the conscientiousness and skill of the magazine's printer. To select the right printer and to work with him as efficiently as possible are important editorial functions. And the final steps in the editorial process concern those tasks that are performed cooperatively with the printing shop. From first plans to first issue is a long road, but the end—a printed issue of your magazine—is now in view.

You know by now that the printing industry has developed in the last fifteen years several new processes of printing. This chapter will describe them briefly so that you can choose among them when making initial decisions about the process and the printing shop you select.

This chapter, however, begins with the editorial tasks necessary if your magazine is printed by letterpress—for many years the only one available, and for some years the standard one.

You should be ready at this time to send to your printer all copy, and cuts if you deal directly with the engraver, for a complete issue of your magazine. At this point in the process, time has become even more pressing than in earlier stages. Even if you are ready exactly on your printer's deadline, as you should be, you should deliver your copy as quickly as possible. If you and your printer are located in the same town, delivery is easy. Most printers maintain a messenger service and will call for your copy at an agreed-upon time or upon a call from you by telephone. Otherwise, you should find another way of delivering the copy by hand.

If your printer is located in another town, you must trust to the mail. Find out at what time of day you must have your copy at the post office to receive the best service, and work toward that precise deadline. The manuscript copy and the dummy must go by first-class mail, but the engravings, in the event the printer is not responsible for having them made, may go by parcel post. If your book is of fairly large size, this mailing cost may be a substantial item. If so, investigate the cost of sending the whole package by express. It is usually slower, but you may be able to work out an arrangement for special handling.

❧ PROOFREADING

The next time you see this issue of your magazine, it will be in the form of page proof. Each page or facing pages, with pictures and text, will be shown printed on a separate proof sheet. If you use color, the color plates on each page will also be shown on a proof sheet separate from the black; however, they will be proved in black. Some printers prove the color plates on tissue and attach them to the proofs of the black plates, showing how the black and the color will be superimposed. In either case, you can see how they match up by holding the pages to the light and adjusting them so that one page is exactly over the other. The printer will also return the copy and the dummy.

The proof sheets may be thought of as a trial run of the magazine. All the text has been set in metal type, which has been combined with the cuts (photoengravings) on forms according to the specifications on your dummy. The forms have been inked and an impression made on sheets of proof paper, not the stock on which the book will eventually be printed. You can now see approximately what the issue is going to look like when printed. This is the time in the editorial process for reading proof, an editorial routine that we turn to now.

WHAT TO LOOK FOR. One of the first things you will notice when you begin reading and checking proofs is whether or not your fitting has been accurate. If the manuscript copy made more lines of type than you had calculated, the extra lines in each case will be printed in the margin of the proof sheet, showing that the text more than filled the page. These lines are known as overset. If the reverse is the case, the page will show a hole of white space or a hole filled with what the printer calls dead metal, that is, metal to fill the column but which will not be used when the form is run on the press. If you made up your dummies from galley proofs, the fitting should be accurate at this stage. If you estimated your copy, not using galleys, the fitting should not be off by more than three or four lines on any page. Large holes or large amounts of overset show that you have made a mistake either in making up the dummy or in estimating the copy. It is also possible that the printer may not have followed the specifications on the dummy, although this is less likely. Even so, you should check the proof sheets against the dummy, especially to see if the white spaces have been inserted as indicated. Sometimes printers will "squeeze" the white space around titles and blurbs in order to get all the type lines on a page to avoid overset. It is better, however, from your viewpoint, to preserve the allotted white space as planned and take care of the overset in one of the ways described below. When the printer understands that the amount of white space was carefully considered and when your specifications on the dummy are perfectly clear, he will follow your wishes.

You will also look for typographical errors. For this, you must read the proof word by word. Pay especially close attention to titles, blurbs, by-lines, and captions. Proofreaders are noted for finding obscure mistakes in the text and overlooking one in the big type of the headline. Notice punctuation, especially parentheses and quotation marks. The errors that occur most frequently are transposed letters and letters dropped out of words. Sometimes a line of the manuscript will have been omitted, or a line of type will be out of place. Work from a first-class printing shop will show a minimum of these typographical errors, since it is customary for the proof to be read from copy by the printer's proofreaders. In the printing shop, usually one person reads aloud the copy while another checks the proof. Most of the typesetter's errors will have been caught in this process. However, this should not relieve the editorial office of reading proof.

The typesetter's rule is to "follow copy." Therefore any errors or carelessness in your copy will be perpetuated in the proof. As you read, you may find instances of faulty hyphenization, capitalization, or punctuation which should have been corrected in the copy. The general policy is that you do not do copyreading on proof, chiefly because all the changes you make constitute an additional printing expense. Your contract with the printer will allow you a certain amount for corrections, called alterations, but when they become excessive, your printing costs will increase. The expert editor has his copy in the best shape possible before he sends it to the printer. Nevertheless, when slips in copyreading make the text confusing to the reader, they should be corrected in proof; but if they are purely technical in character, they probably should stand as they are. For example, incomplete quotation marks hinder the reader's understanding, but a misplaced hyphen will pass unnoticed.

MAKING ALTERATIONS. The first thing to understand in making alterations in proof is that you are not correcting a manuscript as in copyreading, but giving directions for changes in lines of type cast in metal. In letterpress printing, the type is cast by a typesetter operating a Linotype machine. Occasionally a Monotype machine, which follows a different process, is used, but the result in lines of type is the same. As the name implies, the Linotype machine sets one line at a time in solid metal and stacks the lines in order; its operator presses keys on a keyboard which looks something like that of a typewriter. Typesetting is called composition, and is one of the chief charges in letterpress printing. Visualizing lines of type metal rather than printed lines will help you in handling proofs.

All notations on a proof sheet should be legible. They should be made with a colored pencil, never with pen and ink. Choose a color that is different from the one used by the printer's proofreader. The proofreader should be thoroughly familiar with proofreaders' marks, fairly standardized symbols for instructions to the printer which would otherwise have to be written out. All corrections must be made in the margin opposite the line of type to be corrected. If more than one change is made in a single line, the alterations should be indicated in the order in which they appear in the type line. The marks should be separated by diagonal lines. Do not make any marks in the type line itself that will render it illegible, for the printer must be able to identify the location of each change and understand quickly the alteration called for. A good policy is to circle the letter or word to be changed or deleted and to use a caret to indicate where an insert is to be made. Make your marks in the margin clear and bold, so they will not be overlooked. Guide lines from corrections in the margin to type lines are not usually helpful; use them only when absolutely necessary and never have them cross. (Most stylebooks and some dictionaries include a list of proofreaders' marks with illustrations of the manner in which they are applied.)

Remember that each line is cast on one slug, a solid piece of metal. The slightest alteration in a line calls for the whole slug to be reset. Remember also that a line of type can hold only a certain number of characters. If the number of characters in a line is to be changed, not only will that line have to be reset, the remaining lines which follow in the same paragraph will all probably have to be reset. (The typesetter may possibly be able to add or subtract one character, perhaps two, by making the spaces between words narrower or wider.) Editors try to prevent resetting, or new composition, because it is costly. When it is necessary to change a line, make an effort to preserve the number of characters, so that only one line must be reset. It is not always possible to do this, but resourcefulness in this respect is characteristic of the expert proofreader.

When you have indicated all the necessary corrections in the text, you are ready to do the final fitting, that is, to take care of any holes or overset that appears on the pages.

As was suggested above, you first check the proofs against the dummy to make sure that the page layouts have been followed accurately. You may find, when you see a particular layout in proof, that it does not work out successfully, that is, it does not look as effective as you had anticipated. Possibly some shifts in position of pictures or type masses will improve the appearance of the page. It is not too late to make adjustments of this kind; indicate with arrows on the proof sheet exactly the changes you desire. Sometimes by such shifts a hole will be filled because the page has been opened up or an overset will be absorbed because the page has been made tighter. Be sure to count the lines placed in each column of your new layout in order to have an exact fit. If your changes are complicated, you should supply the printer with a new dummy, so that he can see quickly how to remake the page. You should not, of course, change the size of pictures, since that would require new engravings.

Although changes in layouts are practicable, they are not the best practice. An additional charge will be made unless the changes are covered by the allowance for alterations in the printer's contract. You should be able to visualize the appearance of the pages from the dummy, so that new layouts at the proof stage will not be necessary—one reason for making the layouts exact in the first place. Experience in handling layouts will sharpen your power of visualization.

In most cases fitting should be done without remaking the page. From the standpoint of the printer, the easiest way to handle overset is to delete the required number of lines. In cutting lines in proof, you must again keep in mind that you are eliminating whole lines of metal type, not words from a manuscript. Always cut from the ends of paragraphs, never from the middle. The printer can then take out the proper number of lines without having to reset more than the new last line of the paragraph.

If you have a page with many lines of overset, read each paragraph to see whether one or more lines can be eliminated at the end without sacrificing content. Notice especially the paragraph with a short last line. Possibly cutting one word, such as an adjective or an adverb, from the next to the last line will pull the word, or words, of the last line back, thus eliminating a line. Try to locate end-of-paragraph sentences that do not add anything to the sense or information of the article. However, do not cut the connective sentence, that is, the one which leads the reader into the next paragraph.

After you have deleted the required number of lines, you must show how the type lines are to be shifted so that each column will be filled. For example, if a page has two columns, and two lines have been deleted from the first column because there were two lines of overset shown at the end of the second, indicate with a bracket or an arrow, or both, that the top two lines of column two are to be transferred to the bottom of column one. Some proofreaders also write these directions in the margin. Be sure also to show how lines are to be moved from one page to another—that is, which lines are to be transferred, and where they are to be inserted— when a deletion is made on one page to absorb an overset on another.

Let us assume that you have a ten-line overset on page 3 and that you have a hole of about the same size on page 6. You should not fill the hole by making a jump out of the extra lines, a practice which is haphazard and nonprofessional and which would give your book a ragged appearance. If you follow the practice of continuing articles on the back pages, these jumps should be as carefully planned and estimated as the text on the front pages. Any overset would of course show up on the jump page.

To fill the hole on page 6, you add lines to the ends of paragraphs, in the reverse of the process of cutting. Possibly you can add a blurb to the page and adjust the columns accordingly. If the hole is on the second page of an article which happens also to be a left-hand page, you might devise a brief filler which may or may not have anything to do with the article. It does not have to go at the end of the page. Place it wherever it will look well with other items on both the same page and the opposite right-hand page. Here is an opportunity to use one of the brief spots described earlier, possibly something in color. In filling a hole, the existing lines of the columns must be counted and exactly adjusted in the same manner described for the situation which called for cutting.

The difficulty of cutting and filling and the time involved emphasize the wisdom and value of accurately estimating copy. It is much easier to fit manuscript copy than it is to make alterations in proof. Give yourself time to make revisions at the manuscript stage rather than waiting until you are confronted with awkward situations in proof.

Occasionally a proof page will show a short end-of-paragraph line at the top of a column. Printers call it a "widow," and their proofreader will likely mark it "fill," because it looks unsightly on a page. It is your job to fill out the line to the right-hand margin, which is usually very easy to do.

Unless your book is a very simple operation, you should receive a second proof which will show the appearance of the pages after all the alterations have been made. At this point everything should be in order, and only simple checking should be necessary. If this is not the case, it probably means that you made mistakes in calculations or overlooked items on the first proof. The second proof is not provided for an editor to do second-guessing. Therefore, no change of any substance should be made, because it is too close to press time.

Do not change your mind about alterations. This is the moment to let things stand. Learn from any mistake you have made by handling future issues better. The printer will want the editor's okay on this second proof as quickly as possible so that he can lock up the forms and start the press rolling.

✤ PROOF SCHEDULES

If you sent your copy to the printer on your deadline, you should receive the proof pages also on the agreed-upon deadline. A schedule for the movement of copy and proof is one of the important understandings you have with the printer. You cannot meet your distribution or mailing date without a firm schedule, which both you and the printer must follow conscientiously. Sample schedules were shown in Chapter 1.

Accordingly, when proof is received in an editorial office, it should be handled immediately, because the schedule is tighter as you move toward the end of the editorial process. Also, if you are conscientious about meeting your deadlines, you are in a better position to hold the printer to his deadlines. In any case, deadlines should not be allowed to lapse without consultation. If you foresee that you will be late with copy, you should warn the printer so that he can adjust his work load if possible. Similarly, if he falls behind schedule in sending proof, you are justified in inquiring about it.

It is well to arrange schedules so that you do not have a copy deadline for one issue and a proof deadline for the next one at the same time. If, however, you have fallen behind in your schedules and you are faced with both jobs simultaneously, it is better to give the proof priority, because there is more chance to make up lost time on the copy than on the proof. It is especially important to handle a second proof at once, probably in a matter of hours.

Keeping to schedules makes it necessary occasionally to work under pressure. This may mean long or late hours for some people, and editorial workers should understand this necessity. If it turns out that the pressure is continuous, it probably means that the work load is too heavy for the size of the staff.

❖ RELATIONS WITH THE PRINTER

The editor, his executive, and the printer are all interested in making the magazine look and be its best. The printer is usually as concerned as you are in this effort, because he wants to please his customer and also because he has pride in his craft. Some cooperation from you will make him better able to do his best work.

For example, you should guard against making impractical or unreasonable demands. Do not make needless alterations on proofs, and keep those you do make as simple as possible. If you do not know the amount of work involved in a change, you can always inquire. Often the printer will be able to suggest the most practical way of accomplishing your purpose. Furthermore, you should not ask for rush work except in a real emergency. Do not delay reading proof and then expect the printers to work overtime in order to meet the schedule. Keeping to time schedules will greatly facilitate your dealings with the printer.

Try to learn as much as you can about printing processes

so you can do your work with intelligence and dispatch. You will find it interesting to visit the printing shop, especially at a time when your magazine is running on the press, which in a sense is the climax of the editorial process.

At the same time, there are certain things you may reasonably expect of your printer. Primary among these is good printing. The following are some of the marks of good letter press printing which you may watch for.

First, care in following your directions, especially if you have consulted the printer about the best way of giving those directions. You can easily adhere to any preferences he may have in this matter.

Second, skillful typesetting. Notice in the proof whether the type lines are well justified. "Justifying" lines means making them come out even at the right-hand margin, which the typesetter accomplishes by adjusting the spaces between words. These spaces should be neither too wide nor too narrow. They should give a uniform tone to a column of type, so that the reader is not conscious of them. Sometimes the lines are so poorly justified that a river of white space runs down the column. You should call attention to it on the proof.

Third, expert presswork. You can judge presswork only from the printed copies. The impression of the type on the paper should be sharp and uniform in tone; some columns should not be grayer or dimmer than others. The reproductions of the photographs should look clear and contrasty, not a smudgy gray. The full-tone colors should look solid and not show watery places or white specks, which may be the result of faulty inking of the rollers of the press. The pages should be assembled properly, so that the margins of facing pages align exactly; in other words, the printed matter across the top of a two-page spread should make a straight line. The book should be properly trimmed, so that the margins are correct.

You may also expect that the printer will consistently use the kind and quality of paper agreed upon. He should consult with you if any change is necessary. Prompt service and meeting of deadlines are requirements you may insist upon, although, as was indicated above, the printer's ability to meet his deadlines may depend upon the way you meet yours.

It is inevitable, but also fortunate, that you will have many consultations with the printer, or his representative, face to face and over the telephone. Getting your book expertly printed is a job you do together, and the more times difficulties can be worked out cooperatively, the better it is for you, for the printer, and for your magazine.

❧ OFFSET PRINTING

To this point in this chapter we have assumed that your magazine will be printed by the process called letterpress, which has had a long history in printing. It grew out of the invention of printing by means of movable type (take your choice between the ancient Chinese and Gutenberg as the first to use it) and has been so much improved through the centuries that it has been used almost exclusively until quite recently. When well handled, the reproduction by letterpress printing is not only very satisfactory but also beautiful. The previous pages must have demonstrated to you how complicated a process it is, and the number of people involved. And today it has become very expensive.

If you remember back to the Introduction, you will recall that another process was referred to there and elsewhere as rising in popularity using photography as the main printing process. It is called offset.

Offset, the popular name for photolithography, is a planographic process (as contrasted to the *relief* printing of letterpress) in which the images of the letters and pictures are transferred photographically to a flat, thin, metal plate which has been chemically treated so that certain areas receive ink and others resist it. The term "offset" comes from the fact that the impression on paper is not direct from plate to paper; the ink on the plate is transferred to a rubber "blanket" or roll which in turn transfers it to paper.

Type matter to be printed by offset, whether in combination with illustrations or not, may be set by machine as in letterpress printing. Another process, once thought not to be for the small magazine but now both readily available and economically feasible, is computer typesetting. Covered at the conclusion of this chapter, photocomposition and offset printing today are not only inseparable but also financially practical.

Or, if these are too expensive, the type matter may be composed on one of the new office typewriting machines. By "typewriting machine" I do not mean the old portable Royal you used in college. Go visit the IBM sales department in your town. If there is not one in your town, there will be one not more than 100 miles away.

It is a cliché of the marketplace that IBM developed its

business by keeping its mind on its customers as much as on its patents and technology. Distribution is the word, so you will be welcomed. The first thing you will notice is that everything is run by electricity. And typists can now preserve their fingernails attractively curved and polished. The keys of an electric typewriter are not pounded but pressed lightly. There are IBM machines, spawned by the old-fashioned typewriter, that justify lines (make the right side of the column even), correct their own mistakes, offer a variety of type styles and sizes, and do any number of other things. Not every machine does all these things. Instead of buying a new font of type the printer buys one or more balls (literally, they look like Christmas tree ornaments) any one of which, when attached to this new type of machine, will supply a style and size of type to your needs. Inside these little balls (some golf ball size, some larger), is a mechanism that produces print-like copy on paper while you type away as on the ordinary typewriter keyboard. It is a substitute for that curve of keys that used to mess you up so often. One more plug, as it were: your old typewriter was either elite or pica type (each a certain number of spaces to a pica or an inch), and remained that way. The new machine we are describing is equipped with something called "pitch." Say you have set your "pitch" at twelve spaces to the inch. When you have reached a certain point on the page you realize there will be a blank space at the bottom of the column—very awkward. It is not going to fill. So you change your pitch by pressing a lever and your copy will come out at ten spaces to the inch, thereby absorbing the unwanted space at the bottom. We defy any average reader to detect that anything has been manipulated.

The next step is to retype your copy in what is called a "camera ready" form. You now will see the full advantages of your new machine. You have attached the ball that has been selected for the body type, and you have calculated the number of lines your copy will make on your new machine. It may be more or less than the copy as typed by the author. It is the same kind of fitting you do when converting the typed version to the printed version of the manuscript for letterpress process. Your new typewriter may almost be said to do the jobs of the typesetter, and the pressmen. The most important consideration is that this new typed copy be *perfect*, not only in such matters as typos, but so that it exactly fits the space and form allowed for it on your dummy. This is often a difficult and specialized job, but remember you have a sophisticated machine. It will correct errors and, within limits, modify the spacing to fit if your calculations have been a little off. Remember, too, that you can always make a second or even a third try.

An experienced typist can learn to use this machine by trial and error and by reading the instructions. It is better, however, to get the IBM demonstrator to help you understand better what you are doing and how to do it.

At this point most printers will consider the editors' job finished and go on from there. He will size the pictures as you indicated and then will mount them and your camera-ready copy on heavy board, according to the dummy you have supplied, usually two facing pages on one board. You can see at this point exactly what your book is going to look like because the small offset machine will photograph as many copies of what is on those boards as you ordered. This

machine is usually quite small, about the size of a large refrigerator but shaped differently. Also it is very different from
even a small letterpress machine. It is also fast and can print
flat color.

This mounting process is very special, so it is usually done
by an expert in the shop, but some editors are skillful enough
to do it. If you can, it will usually cut your printing bill.
However, it is a time-consuming process and the editor may
find that other responsibilities should have priority.

You will not see a proof and at this time no changes of
mind can be made. Some editors consider this such a serious
drawback that they would rather use another process.

One such option is called a minipress and is appropriate
only for the small types of jobs we have been considering. Instead of a platen for printing, the mini-press uses plastic
sheets, and they are for short runs only—300 to 5000 depending on the kind of plastic sheet used. The printing is
clear and sharp. This operation is more akin to letterpress
than offset but is excellent for small jobs. The effect is more
formal than the camera-ready operation but the magazine at
least has "a new look" and suggests the casual and informal
impressions appropriate to some small magazines.

THE BIG OFFSET JOBS. Surveying informally the variety of
small magazines, you see that some of them are very substantial jobs. Let us take three at random: *The Columbia Journalism Review*, 56 pages; *Arizona Highways*, 46 pages; *The
Smithsonian*, 100 pages. They have comparable dimensions,
about 8 x 11 inches. Each of these books would be considered a big printing job but each is also, according to our definition, a small magazine. We do not know the circulation of

any of them but we suspect they are large, with the possible exception of the *Review*.

Now let us go out on a limb and guess the way each one was printed. *The Review* I suspect is an offset job, judging from the reproduction of its photos that are all black and white. *The Review* uses color only on its cover. These photos look fine. They are clear and the blacks and grays show up smoothly. But they have a soft and not a sharp appearance. One difference between letterpress and offset is just this. Even the type in offset printing has a less sparkling look as do the pictures. This is a well-printed magazine very appropriate to its content. Now take a look at *Arizona*, which I am guessing is letterpress, selected because of the many handsome photographs it uses. The colors are clearly separated and give a sharp linear impression. If printed by offset some of the elegant detail might be a little diffused. When a photographer has worked on a single, yellow-flowered cactus plant for a half page picture, he wants each petal to show all the tender lines that make its distinctive shape. So out on this limb I am saying it is a work of letterpress art. Now *The Smithsonian*. For one thing, it prints very different kinds of pictures from *Arizona Highways*. Among other things it reproduces master paintings, old and new, as well as medieval master tapestries. Here the soft look, the diffusion of color (often planned by the artist) is an advantage. Considering also the type impression, I opt for a first class offset job.*

---

* As I said before, I was just guessing about which process was used for each of the three magazines, based on my experiences in the past. As it turns out, all three were done by offset, so appearances can be deceptive, and the possibilities of offset should not be underestimated.

These three instances have been described to indicate the differences in appearance of the reproductions of the two processes. Each has its advantages and disadvantages. For some jobs color printing by offset is likely to be cheaper. In fact, some claims have been made that it is nearly always cheaper. But really that depends on what you want done.

An editor has the same jobs to do in one of these substantial magazines as in the much more numerous small ones discussed above. The only difference is that it will take him longer. It will require even a small staff and he has more decisions to make. The printer and his operators have many steps to take between the time they receive copy and the time the head of the offset department says "We are starting the press at 12:30." But this is not the place to describe them.

The editor will receive a proof, sometimes called a van dyke, in black and white that will give him a general idea of the book but this is not the time for any correction or change of mind, unless some crucial mistake has been made along the line. Such a disaster is very serious, especially for the printer, because he must almost begin again. In a good shop this sort of thing will seldom happen. All shops have (or should have) a person in charge of quality control of the press. He examines minutely the first printed issues to see if the color is consistent with the first "color separations" made for a full color job. Color may be adjusted, though not changed, in the ink rollers while the press is running. Printers have almost a superstition about stopping a big press in the middle of a run unless something dire has happened.

If you have "ink in your blood" you will have fun visiting

various printing shops to watch the presses, small and large, at work. One editor of several small magazines with long runs and liberal use of color said that nothing about his work fascinated him more than watching the enormous (as big as a fair sized room) offset press at work on one of his jobs. He said it looked as if all the pressmen did was stroll around on catwalks on the machine, and press buttons! A huge roll of paper was placed at one end by pressing a button, and his completed magazines came out 30 feet along the line at a speed of 35,000 an hour. He said what was most interesting about the letterpress operation was the process of making the color plates.

❖ PHOTOCOMPOSITION

Today, the most popular method of typesetting with printers and publishers in the U.S. is photocomposition. About 75% to 80% of all printed matter is set this way. As the name implies, this process evolved from photography.

Instead of using huge and costly machines that melt and cast type characters in lead in a process involving hundreds of expensive manual handlings, photocomposition employs a minimum of people, several electronic machines (including a computer), cold paper, and film. Long in development and highly sophisticated during its perfecting, this comparatively simple technique has literally revolutionized the printing and publishing industries at every level.

Here is a simplified description of a typical phototypesetting process:

The editor's manuscript is given a story number, not only

for computer identification all the way to the printed page, but also for quick retrieval from the process at any needed point along the way.

The story is then encoded, that is, programmed for the computer. The coding is uncomplicated, consisting of a series of simple "command" symbols which are written on the manuscript.

A keypunch operator, using an electronic machine that closely resembles a large typewriter, transfers everything in the manuscript—including the commands—onto a paper tape. Though this tape contains no recognizable words, it can be "read" for accuracy by the operator who punched it. In some cases, where a positive reading is desired (for example, of complex mathematical formulas), phototypesetters will employ visual readout machines. The punched tape is run through as the operator scans a CRT (cathode ray tube) screen upon which the actual English words and the technical or mathematical information that requires the extra-close proofing. If errors are found, the tape can be stopped and the errors corrected literally on-screen.

Once "read", the story tape roll is inserted in an electronic reader—a black box measuring 8 inches by 6 inches by 5 inches. The tape is threaded and drawn across a light sensor which transmits everything on it to a computer—the largest piece of equipment in the process yet no larger than one of the old, hot-type Linotype machines. Its measurements: 7 feet by 4 feet by 6 feet.

The computer, which has been previously programmed, responds to all the information on the paper tape. The coding, mentioned before, tells the computer what the size of the type is, what the length of the line is, how much space or "leading" goes between each line, when the type should change from regular to bold face or italic, when to paragraph or indent copy. In short, every instruction that you might give to a human typesetter is received and registered by the computer, a machine that has probably been manufactured in the same plant that once produced scores of the old hot-type machines that did a fraction of the printing—from typesetting to page proofs—that the computer is now capable of handling.

Several products now emerge from the computer. They are: a printout containing the story; a mylar plastic tape on a disc which then becomes a permanent memory storage device; a paper tape that can be used to transmit the story by wire (if the printing plant is distant); a tape that will, when run through a phototypesetting machine on the premises, produce photographic "galleys" of the story.

The story printout can be proofread, corrected, or added to until the author is satisfied. The corrections are keypunched, then fed through the computer and onto the memory storage tape, and these corrections are made simultaneously on all tapes, as well as on the final printout.

The phototypesetting tape is then fed into the setting machine which is roughly the size of a large refrigerator. This machine (cost: $95,000 plus) contains several character discs—wheels made of sandwiched glass that has been laminated. Each disc consists of hundreds of etched type characters—upper and lower case, italics, bolds, and regular faces—

but they are all of one family or face. To change typeface, a disc is removed and a new disc is mounted on the "Ferris wheel" yoke. Each disc, incidentally, costs about $900.

At a rate of roughly 14 lines per minute, the phototypesetter, guided by the tape output, "shoots" light through the type characters etched in the disc and onto sensitized photographic paper on the other side of the machine. The results: positive, black-on-white photographic galleys which are now ready for camera. These galleys, on what is called reproduction proof paper, are then machine copied and sent (with film of illustrations or photos) to be made up into page dummies as per the editor's instruction by the offset department.

Initially, only the machine copies are used, but once the editor has approved the page, the "repro proofs" and illustration film are mounted and photographed. The result, then, is a complete page on one piece of film that is now ready to be printed—either on the premises or at a distant plant.

What's more, the entire process has taken only 25% of the time required by hot-type processes, fewer people and fewer steps are involved, opportunity for error is cut down dramatically and the final product is most impressive in appearance. An added bonus: producing reprints is greatly simplified. The film is easily stored compared to metal type and filmed pages of film pages can be turned out ad infinitum.

Photocomposition can be as practical for small publications as for large. Costs do not vary much nor do they depend so much on quantity as they did in the days of hot-type.

In Chapter 8, "Basic Design," more will be said about selecting the kind of printing process desirable for your own small magazine.

CHAPTER SEVEN

BASIC EDITORIAL POLICY

We have been concerned so far with the day-to-day operations of publishing the small magazine, the editorial process. We have considered the editorial skills and techniques involved in this process, the technical functions. Other editorial functions, however, are equally important in the life of the magazine. These we call "executive functions" because they have to do with decisions fundamental to the entire procedure; such decisions are usually made by the executive or executives of the sponsoring body, not by the editor, although he should participate in them.

We now consider these executive functions which, as a matter of fact, precede and underlie the editor's technical operations. Most technical decisions are made in line with some executive decision already established. After all, these executive matters concern basic editorial policy and general format of the magazine. The day-to-day editorial process is carried forward within these limits. An executive editorial decision is likely to affect and to apply to all issues of a magazine, whereas a technical decision usually concerns one issue or even one feature of an issue. This distinction between the two functions and their relationship to each other will be illustrated in the discussions that follow.

❖ THE NATURE OF BASIC EDITORIAL POLICY

An essential and far-reaching executive function is the establishment of basic editorial policy. Editorial policy is a kind of blueprint of your book that indicates the boundaries within which individual issues are built. In general, the editorial policy sets the purpose of the magazine, determines its character and over-all slant, defines the nature of the content by which the purpose is to be achieved, indicates the special mood or tone desired, and establishes size, number of pages, and frequency of publication.

It should be clear that these decisions must be made before any issue is planned and that they serve as a guide to the editor in his day-to-day operations. When basic editorial policy is clearly articulated, it helps the editor to keep the magazine in line with its purpose and consistent with its message. With such a guide a magazine attains a distinctive profile or personality and becomes an effective instrument of communication. In addition, it frees the editor from the necessity of making policy decisions opportunistically and aids him in differentiating between questions of policy and questions of technique. For example, if there is no policy on illustrations, the editor may accept an article because of good accompanying photographs and the next day accept a second article without photographs with no thought of whether or not it should be illustrated. The result may be that the appearance of his pages would show no consistency, the outlines of the book's profile would be blurred. If the policy of the magazine is to use photographic illustrations, before using the second article the editor would have to decide how it should be illustrated and how he would obtain appropriate photographs. If he cannot do so, he probably should not publish the article, no matter how appropriate it is on other counts. Thus basic policy is a source of discipline as well as freedom for the editor.

It is on policy that the editor is most closely related to his executive or administrator. In a nonconsumer magazine, the person to whom the editor is responsible usually is a staff officer of the sponsoring body, or the head of the department in which responsibility for the publication is lodged. This officer should initiate or at least participate in all decisions on policy, so that he understands and is agreeable to the way in which these basic questions have been worked out. The editor is likewise a party to these decisions. After policy matters have been settled (some of them may be left in an experimental stage, of course), the executive need not—and perhaps should not—be involved in the technical functions by which the editor implements policy. If an executive is not confident that his editor can and will carry out agreed-upon policy, he should find another editor, not attempt to supervise closely the technical editorial operations. The editor on his part should be scrupulous, within reasonable, not legalistic, limits, in adhering to editorial policy. Of course, both parties must understand the difference between executive and technical editorial functions.

In some organizations, it may be appropriate for a nonstaff or volunteer officer to participate in policy making for the organization's journal, for example, the president or chairman in cases where the employed officer is an executive secretary. This is often a good way to make sure the magazine reflects reader interest and to give the readers' elected officers a legitimate role with respect to their magazine. This also serves to cement the relationship between the book and is sponsoring body. At the same time, after policy has been established, volunteer personnel should never be involved in the day-by-day technical functions of the editor. While the counsel of the volunteer may be valuable on such questions as whether the book should appear monthly or quarterly, it will be of little value (and may foul the operations) on such questions as whether this article or that picture should be used. Carrying out editorial policy requires journalistic skills that cannot be expected in the average volunteer. The editor's executive is responsible for protecting him from undue interference and pressure and also for giving the volunteer an opportunity to fulfill his appropriate role.

In some organizations, especially those at a local level, the executive and the editor may be the same person, and he may also be a volunteer. It is then especially important that he understand the nature and function of editorial policy and how this policy is related to his daily operational decisions. He should not confuse in his mind his day-to-day operations with basic policy. Possibly, also, he may invent a practical way to avail himself of the judgment of officers who are directly in touch with his readers. For example, all or part of a meeting of the organization, or, if that would be too cumbersome, the board of directors or executive committee, may be devoted to a consideration of the magazine's policy.

In any case, basic editorial policy should never be up for revision oftener than once a year unless some emergency occurs. It usually takes at least that long to test the validity of a policy decision. In a later section, the subject of changing basic policy is considered.

With editorial planning in mind, you should be aware of the way in which planning is related to basic policy. You will recall that plans are made in the light of the book's purpose, slant, and character. Also, you should be able now to distinguish between editorial planning and the policy-making procedure, although some (not all) of the same people are involved. The distinction will become even clearer as we discuss steps in making policy in the following section.

❖ ESTABLISHING EDITORIAL POLICY

The editorial policy of a small magazine grows out of the purpose and the program of the sponsoring body. If the purpose is to keep the members abreast of the trends and developments in a certain field (for instance, adult education, square dancing, etc.), if it is to work together in an area of mutual interest, such as parents and teachers do in the field of education, if it is to bring together people in a common field of work and to enterprise a cooperative national program, this purpose and the resulting program, through which the purpose is effected, will determine to a large extent the editorial policy of the magazine. The initial question to ask is: what part of our purpose may be achieved by a magazine? And a corollary is: what aspects of our program can be furthered by a magazine?

In answering these questions, keep in mind that a magazine is best used to report, that is, to give information about events and activities or both, about trends and developments in an area of thought; to describe and interpret a point of view; to stimulate interest and concern in a projected or ongoing program; to foster a feeling of mutuality among its readers. These are very significant functions and explain why almost all organizations are quick to get out publications of some sort. They also account for the large number of small magazines. As you think of the way your book can perform these functions for your sponsoring group, that is, as you build editorial policy, you should make the following decisions:

1. Decide exactly who your expected readers are and what they are like. Take into account such matters as sex, age, educational level, economic status, national and cultural background, place of residence. A magazine of a professional women's organization will have a readership quite different in these respects from a publication for employees of an industry or department store. Make a list of the dominant interests of your readers and the chief values they cherish. Then select those that are related to the purpose of your organization. These interests vary widely from group to group, for instance, as between clerical or secretarial employees in a large business and the executive or managerial employees. For this reason some houses have separate publications for the two groups. The nature of your list will depend on the character

of your expected readership, whether it is general and wide-spread or specific and narrowly focused.

2. Keeping in mind your readers and your organization's purpose and program, formulate the purpose and central message of your magazine. What will the magazine say to its readers? What sort of message will it communicate? Let us take some examples.

A house publication distributed to employees who are geographically scattered might well work toward the following purposes: to help its readers to understand the nature and function of the business of which they are a part; to relate themselves intelligently and responsibly to the operations of the business; to comprehend the relation of the company to the business world and to the community in general; to feel personally involved with other employees and with the life of the company.

The magazine of a club, guild, league, or other organization with local units and a national program might serve some such purposes as: to enable the members of the organization, that is, the magazine's readers, to become better informed about the program and work of the total group; to become aware of the meaning and significance of the organization; to understand the way in which the local unit is related to other local units and to feel personally involved with other members in a common effort; to feel that the national body is interested in and concerned about the members as persons, not merely as units of a body; to become more active and more effective participants in the organization.

For a magazine with a local circulation, such as one serving a local or regional unit of a national organization, or a local business, industry, or institution, the following might be the purposes: to acquaint the readers personally with one another; to express common interests as they relate to the sponsoring body; to help the readers to sense the significance and understand the meaning of what they do together and to become informed about their common work and program.

The purposes of the journal serving a professional group or a group with some specialized interest might be stated like this: to voice the common concerns of the readers; to inform them about trends, events, and developments; to facilitate their activity in the field or help them become more able practitioners.

You will notice some common threads running through the statements of purpose of these four categories of magazines. All the purposes are, for the most part, personal in character, and they appeal in some measure to the emotions of the readers. This is due to the fact that the readers of a small magazine are related to one another, in a group which is more or less organized. Therefore, the publication speaks to individuals as they relate to their group life and voices a personal message. In one sense, it is selling the group to the individual, and in another sense, the individual to the group. The several specific purposes, in turn, contribute to one general objective: the building of morale, both individual and collective.

3. In the light of the characteristics of your readership and the purpose you want to accomplish, decide on the general character of your book, its basic slant or personality. This is a part of editorial policy that amateurs often neglect. For ex-

ample, would your magazine best communicate your message with a folksy, casual, and colloquial character or with a dignified and restrained character; or would it implement your purpose most expeditiously with a slant that is dramatic and that makes a strong impact?

The casual character would be appropriate for local readers who are fairly well known to one another or for readers in a restricted nonprofessional field of interest who may be widespread geographically. Magazines on hobbies or avocational interests (for example, astronomy, numismatics, mountaineering), and publications circulating to the employees of a local or closely knit company fall into this category. Informality and humor can be nicely employed here, whereas in other situations they would be out of place.

A dignified tone would obviously be suitable for professional and some scholarly journals. Dignity and restraint, however, should not be considered synonymous with dullness and solemnity. A magazine may be alert, lively, and interesting without sacrificing dignity and restraint. One method of achieving both is through the use of journalistic rather than academic techniques of presentation. Academic conventions are properly employed in classrooms and professional meetings, but journalistic styles, such as are described in this book, might furnish a welcome change of pace in the professional magazine. This does not mean "popularizing" content "down" to the mass level, but it does mean making it more readily communicable and more closely related to human values and experience. For this reason, the editor might well be in some cases a professional journalist rather than an expert in the discipline itself.

The magazine with strong dramatic impact is especially suited to a large, widespread constituency such as the membership of a national organization with local units or the employees of a business or industry with decentralized departments or branches. Here, the readers are more likely to resemble the general public than are those of other types of small magazines. By the same token, the book is somewhat in competition with the commercial magazine—not directly, but in the sense that it must claim the reader's attention away from other interests. The reader does not have the sense of intimacy and personal involvement that obtains in the local or specialized constituency. The editorial policy, therefore, must call for the popular and provocative approach, which is not to say the magazine should be sensational or in poor taste. A larger budget may be required for a magazine of this type, although it is not as important as a clear understanding of policy and an editorial expertise in carrying out the policy.

Local or regional units of national organizations may well have their own magazines of an entirely different character (possibly like those of the first category given above) that would not at all parallel the magazine distributed on the national level—this illustrates exactly the necessity for making a decision on slant as a part of editorial policy.

4. Now you are ready to describe the general types of content by which you will achieve your purpose. Content is the means to your ends. Here you are not making specific suggestions for features in a given issue or over a given period of time as in a planning conference; you are describing categories of features which make up your over-all content within which specific items will be planned in the regular ed-

itorial process. The establishment of these general categories is an executive function; planning individual issues is a technical function.

Here is a list of general categories of content, all of which arc appropriate to the small magazine, although any given book is not likely to use all of them. You may choose from among them and think of examples in each case in the light of your particular magazine.

The informative article

The personal experience story—the it-happened-to-me account

The biography or personality profile of someone either living or dead

The informal essay

Reports of findings, events, activities

Interpretation of concepts, trends, developments

Standing departments: the editorial, the column of personal comments, news items, reviews of books, suggested resources for program building, reader contributions

The how-to-do-it piece, that is, instructions, directions, counsel, or advice about readers' activities, relationships, and experiences appropriate to the message of your book

Fiction, appropriate to a few types of small magazines but not usual

At this point you also decide whether or not your book will be illustrated and, if so, how. Explore the uses of photographs and kinds of art work in the light of your purpose and constituency. Your selected categories of content are also a factor in this decision on illustrations. It is safe to say that most small magazines should be illustrated. Even the four-page fold, 8½ x 11 inches, or eight-page book in a smaller size, especially if printed by the letterpress method, can use two or more well-planned photographs or a number of pen and ink decorative spots. Probably the magazine of ideas or the scholarly journal would be the only exception. Most non-consumer magazines seek to make a popular appeal, as shown in the discussion of purpose, and pictures are currently in the popular mode.

5. Decide the important question of frequency of publication—weekly, biweekly or fortnightly, monthly, bimonthly, quarterly. A rough-and-ready principle is that the more intimate and colloquial your book, the more frequently it should be published. Local publications, therefore, are generally more effective if the period between issues is not long. Purpose is achieved more effectively by a small publication that reaches the readers often than a more ambitious one that arrives infrequently. The weekly or biweekly may be considered in this case.

The book with a wider constituency is probably most effective if issued monthly. This is quite a common type, because it comes out at intervals well established in the reader's mind and often enough so that interest does not sag between issues. Bimonthly publication is not on the whole very useful. It does not build expectancy among its readers like the magazine which arrives every month, with the result that it is easy for the reader to forget about it between issues. Probably the quarterly achieves a magazine's purpose as well as the magazine which appears six times a year.

The method of distribution is an important factor in deciding frequency of issue. If the book does not have to be mailed, there is no acute problem. Distribution by mail, however, is costly and may constitute a major budget item. You may find in estimating your total cost that the expense of distributing a weekly is prohibitive and therefore decide upon a biweekly. The same consideration might weight a decision in favor of a quarterly instead of a monthly. On the other hand, you may decide the more frequent issue will accomplish so much more that the increased cost of distribution is justified.

6. If you are starting a magazine, you must, of course, give it a name. The current vogue calls for short, even one-word, names for magazines. Also, the trend is away from names with a moralistic tone, like *The Beacon* or *The Crusader*. Names preceded by "the" are also not used as much as formerly.

Keep in mind the following points in selecting a name. The word or words should be euphonious and easy to say, and should if possible fit smoothly into a sentence, for example: "The next issue of ——— will contain . . ." or "Pass out copies of ——— at the meeting." The name should be readily recognized by the readers and perhaps the general public as pertaining to the sponsoring body. For the same reason, an insignia or a symbol of the organization or something pertinent to its history is often selected for the name of its publication. It may or may not be good for the name to designate the readers: it is good if the readers agree to and like the designation, but it is not good if they would not so designate themselves. The name should wear well; it should sound appropriate after five or ten years, unless the life of the magazine is expected to be short. A concrete word is usually to be preferred over an abstract one. This is one advantage also of using an insignia, which has the further advantage of possessing pictorial value.

An organization may arrange a contest or some other device for allowing members to name their magazine, a plan that may have public relations value.

Remember that a magazine is identified with its name in the minds of its readers and that it should therefore strike them as appropriate and pleasing. The name should not be changed once it has been established. Changing a magazine's name amounts to killing it. Therefore, if you want continuity in the life of your publication, preserve its name even though you may radically change its policy. It may be that you have a publication which for some reason has not been successful and is not popular with your constituency, and you want to remake its basic policy along lines that you believe will increase its standing. In this situation, you might well change the name, because in effect you will be establishing a new publication which should not carry for the reader the onus of the former one. The new name will also underline the new character of the magazine.

If your periodical is of considerable size, works toward a significant purpose, and expects to maintain its life over a long period of time, you should register its name with the United States Patent Office. This registration will allow you the sole right to this name. At the same time, you can learn whether the name you propose has already been registered and therefore is not one you can use. When a name is registered, the magazine of that name must be published or the registration becomes void. In other words, you cannot hold a name in reserve. The titles of books, which are neither patented nor copyrighted, do not have the same legal standing as names of magazines. There is no legal restriction against using a book title as the name of a magazine, provided it is not already preempted for magazine use.

✤ CHANGING EDITORIAL POLICY

Once you have made the decisions listed above, you have formulated the basic policy of your magazine, but that does not mean you have settled it forever. You have settled it for such a period of time as will allow you to evaluate its effectiveness. It is quite probable that within a couple of years you will feel that a change is desirable. A useful principle for changing basic policy is that is should always be done gradually, because readers love the familiar. If you want to shift the slant in some way, do not do it all at once, but inch up on it. You will not then disturb the readers who like your book as it is, and at the same time you will be pleasing readers who feel a change necessary. You can, in this way, also keep the magazine up to date. A successful magazine never appears to change. A gradual change which is not readily apparent when it is taking place shows up dramatically when one compares issues five or more years apart.

An editor should not allow himself to run on momentum for very long, nor to let his book sink into a rut. Take the long-range view and estimate the effectiveness of your magazine over a period of years. Be alert to changes that will keep abreast of your readers and your times, but make them slowly, year by year. An editor should always be striving for changes in basic policy, but never seem to do so to his readers. The readers should find the magazine continually appealing without being aware of any great changes. The exception would be when you want to change abruptly an unpopular or ineffective policy. Do not be slow about correcting mistakes, nor ride too long on successes.

Perhaps you are the new editor of a magazine with a long-established policy. It is almost certain that you will be eager to make immediate changes. That is all to the good, because your fresh viewpoint is an advantage. But unless you have been hired expressly to revamp the policy in a hurry, you should control your impulses and make changes slowly, item by item, never all at once. Remember that your readers like the familiar personality of their magazine and do not want to be confronted next month by a total stranger. You can begin immediately in a small way and build major changes gradually. The major changes which you have in view should be cleared in the regular way with your executive and others responsible for policy.

✤ FINANCIAL POLICY

Financial policy is tied closely to circulation, which should be predicted as exactly as possible. Most small magazines enjoy a controlled circulation, that is, the readers are members of groups whose numbers are known or can be estimated in advance. Some groups, a business or a club, may want to use their journals for purposes of publicity or public relations, for which an added number would be printed. It is always a good idea to have a reasonable surplus for various editorial uses. The number of copies per issue may or may not remain the same, but a prediction of long-range circulation should be made so as to establish a probable budget figure for production.

House publications circulating to such groups as employees, dealers, customers, and stockholders are given away and therefore do not bring any income. They are supported by subsidies. Nonconsumer magazines of another type receive an income from a portion of the dues of members of the sponsoring bodies. A smaller number, usually those of public institutions or agencies, are sold to the general public. Except in the case of house publications, it is good policy to charge for your magazine for the reason that people place more value on something they pay for than on something they get free. A price also gives your book a more professional character. Of course, your magazine should impress the reader as being well worth the rate you charge; in fact it may be worth more and require a subsidy in addition to subscription fees. The necessity for such a subsidy will depend partly on your circulation. Generally, the higher the circulation, the less the unit cost is likely to be. Editorial charges against the budget remain the same and production cost per unit goes down as the printing run gets larger. The sponsoring body may wish to keep the subscription rate low, even if it means a subsidy, in order to have the message of its magazine obtain as wide a readership as possible.

An annual budget may include all or some of the following items: manuscripts; illustrations, both photographs and art work; production, that is, printing and engravings; distribution, including postage, envelopes or wrapping, and addressing; salaries of editorial employees; overhead that may be charged against the magazine, including rent, office services, and supplies. Some of these items may not be present in a small operation. For example, overhead may be absorbed in the total budget of the organization. Many house publications are not mailed. The editor may be a volunteer and the only person connected with the magazine, or salaries may be covered by another budget. The content may be staff-prepared, so that no budget is necessary for manuscripts and illustrations. But production and possibly distribution remain budget items that are not likely to be cared for in any other way.

The particular items in your budget and their exact amounts will depend upon circumstances and the nature of your publication. You should recognize, however, that magazine costs includs all the above items, no matter how many of them may be paid for in some way that does not constitute a charge against the magazine.

A firm budget should be established and reviewed annually by the editor and the responsible executive. The editor should feel assured that the contracts he will make with printers, authors, illustrators, and others have adequate financial backing. In turn he should tailor his operations to stay within the established budget except in situations of emergency, which, of course, require executive action. The editorial office may handle its own bookkeeping, in which case the editor should make financial reports at regular intervals to the appropriate executive. If the bookkeeping is done by a central department of the parent body, the editor should receive regular reports of accumulated expenditures against the various budget items.

No magazine should operate on a hand-to-mouth basis with respect to its finances. A publication that is worth producing and putting into the hands of a group of readers is worth a sound financial policy, no matter how simple. The editor may properly take the initiative in this matter if it is neglected or overlooked by his colleagues.

❈ LEGAL MATTERS

All publishing involves certain legal matters with which the editor should be familiar.

Every magazine except the most simple and casual variety should be copyrighted. To copyright a publication is to make a legal registration of its contents, so as to insure that they will not be reproduced in any form without the consent of the owner of the reproduction rights. Otherwise, any person may print all or any part of the contents for any purpose whatever. A magazine that is edited with care for a serious purpose is valuable property and deserves the legal protection of a copyright.

Copyright registrations in the United States are held by an office of the Library of Congress. To copyright a magazine send two copies of *each* issue as soon as it is off the press, before publication date, to the Register of Copyrights, Library of Congress, Washington, D.C., together with the fee of four dollars and a properly executed application form. A supply of these forms will be sent by the Library of Congress on request. When the application has been approved, the Register's office sends a certificate of registration, which constitutes legal proof of copyright. Each issue of the publication carries a copyright notice naming the publisher and the year—for example: Copyright 1958 by Walden Sons & Mott, Inc. This statement is often combined with the postal notice.

The other side of the copyright arrangement comes into play when an author or an editor wants to quote from another copyrighted publication. The United States copyright law allows the free quotation of not more than two sentences of prose. This regulation is waived only in the case of quotations from a book in a responsible and bona fide review of that book. It is illegal to reprint anything from a copyrighted publication in any other circumstances without written permission from the person or institution that owns the publication rights. Ignorance of the fact that a publication is protected by copyright does not constitute a defense. The person or institution owning the publication rights may or may not be the one in whose name the publication has been copyrighted. To copyright a piece of printed matter does not imply or assure rights of reproduction. It is only a legal protection against unauthorized reprinting, or piracy, as it is called in the publishing business.

Published matter may be copyrighted under United States law for twenty-eight years. At the end of that time the copyright may be renewed for another twenty-eight years, after which the material is said to be in the public domain. "In the public domain" means the rights belong to the public, and anyone who may wish to do so is authorized to reissue the publication.

Editors of small magazines should watch their quotations closely and make sure they are within the law. The smart editor also will be suspicious of any author, himself included, who is inclined to quote liberally from other writers without sound justification. This habit may indicate an inability to express himself in his own words, and it encourages the dubious cut-and-paste method of "writing."

The law with regard to libel is another concern of editors. This law protects every citizen against damage sustained by what is said about him in public print. In general, the libel laws provide that a publisher may not legally print anything about a person that would tend to damage him in the eyes of right-thinking people unless the publisher can prove that what he has printed is true. If the publisher is sued, he, the defendant, must prove in court that he printed only the truth, or he is liable for damages. It is a good policy not to print the kind of material that has to be carefully scanned for a risk of libel. Such stories are likely to be inappropriate anyway.

Any periodical using the mails desires a second-class mailing permit, which allows mailing at a lower postal rate. This permit is obtained on request and on meeting the requirements from the postmaster of the office from which the magazines will be mailed. This request should be made while policy is being established and before the first issue is in print. One requirement is that a postal notice be printed on one of the first four pages of the magazine in each issue. The exact wording will be supplied by the post office. It may appear in small type at the bottom of a page and may be combined with the copyright notice. If there is no editorial page, as such, the imprimatur may also be placed here. This is the statement giving the name and address of the publisher and the name of the editor. Names of other responsible persons, such as assistant editor and art editor, may be included if desired.

In addition to basic policy, one other group of executive decisions remains to be made before the magazine can begin publication. These concern the over-all design and are treated in the next chapter.

CHAPTER EIGHT

BASIC DESIGN

The basic design of a small magazine consists of those elements of appearance that remain more or less constant. No matter how spontaneous the rest of the piece may be, the over-all design should remain the same; otherwise the reader may not recognize his old friend. It is as if you built each issue by starting all over again. Starting over again is certainly possible and sometimes necessary. If any of you are old enough to remember the first issue of *Holiday*, you may remember also that the second issue looked very different. The story in the trade was that the inside of the book was so confused, amateurish, and self-conscious that everyone was screaming—the publisher, the advertisers, and the readers.

When the second issue appeared, all was changed for the better. The page size or format and the title remained the same. Some different names appeared on the masthead, so apparently some heads had rolled. I am not referring to the present *Holiday*, which has made recent changes (smaller format among others) evidently in the interest of ecomony.

❧ MAKING DECISIONS ON DESIGN

Basic design is closely related to basic policy, although the same people may not be involved. If you are the only staff member and do all the work yourself you should have advice from several sources, including your supervisor or the president of the organization, and a professional designer. You may have to pay a fee to this last person, but it is well worth the money even if your operation is quite small.

As the editor of the magazine (you may just be starting on your first issue) you have a clear idea of the slant, purpose, and message. You interpret these matters clearly to the president or head. In fact, he should have consulted with you in advance of this consultation so that you are reasonably in agreement about them. It is the president's responsibility to explain a little about the organization and briefly describe what the readers are like, and also the ways in which they are different from one another.

It is the designer's role to think of a variety of ways in which this information may be used in building the basic design.

The elements which go into these decisions on design are: the title, the size of page, both trim size and printed size, the number of pages, the printing process to be used, distribution (will it be mailed?), frequency of issue, a detached or self-cover—all in addition to the purpose as stated above. A local organization of about 500 persons interested in the education of the blind need a newsletter for announcements, for communication among members, for information on trends and developments in their area of concern; they do not require a magazine. Their newsletter could easily be two or even one legal size sheet, mimeographed well and folded and perhaps stapled. It should be a self-mailer with space for imprint, postal notice, and the address of the reader. These readers are an excellent example of the captive audience. They are interested in the content, which is seldom of the kind that they must be cajoled into reading.

On the other hand, your small magazine may be a house organ for a large industry with 35,000 employees living all over the country and a sizable number of outsiders interested in the firm's products and its field. For these readers you require a book of some size, and all the elements mentioned above will apply. It may be that the book is affluent enough to hire a staff designer (who might double as a photographer) and an editorial secretary for the editor.

ABOUT TITLES. It is a strange thing that the title of the magazine may be the last thing to be decided. Some comments were made about titles in Chapter 7. We might just add here that it should not be ambiguous, and it should have some come-on quality. Since it will appear on the cover of every issue it should wear well. It may name in some way the group it represents. *The Omaha Teacher* would be one such but neither euphonious nor interesting. What would you think of *The Three R's?* The latter would lend itself to clever treatment by using an Arabic numeral 3 and lower case r's. It has the limitation that the phrase itself is such a cliché. Maybe the meaning would be identified even more by including "In Omaha" as a small subtitle size.

Examine what other magazines do. *Lancet* seems a good title for a small magazine published by doctors in England.

The single concrete word, if appropriate, is always a good idea. *Think,* published by IBM, seems too abstract and also didactic. Wouldn't you feel like asking "Why?"

Use of an organization's insignia if a visually good one might be played around with. One large bank has one so well known in its city that it could be used alone but then what would you call the magazine? *Fish and Stream* has appeal but *Earth* is ambiguous and at present over-used. For a house organ, what about *The People at the General.* The General is the name of a hospital and could be printed as a small subtitle. The book would be called *The People.*

FORMAT. The word format is sometimes used to include not only the magazine's dimensions and number of pages but also its layouts and even general program. Here, however, the term is used in its limited sense.

The 8 x 11 inch size is still popular with consumer magazines—*House and Garden* and *Newsweek,* for example. Some cling to the large size—*House Beautiful* and *Fortune,* for example. But the large format has been abandoned by many publishers. The pocket book size has lost favor too, with the persistent exception of the *Reader's Digest.* Number of pages in nearly all magazines has been reduced because of the fall-off in ads, and hence income. The steeply climbing cost of production, especially labor and paper, is also a factor.

The small magazine has been seriously affected, too, but in some different ways. Some firms have abandoned their house organs in a time of slow, tight money. If one of them is tied to a strong organization with members, the magazine is likely to go ahead as usual unless membership falls significantly. Because so many small magazines are supported by subsidy they are in a different category from the commercial book.

All these matters will be in the minds of people who are running a small magazine. Before tackling the subject of format, let us pause to consider the general trends in design. Some comments were made on this subject in Chapter 5, "Hints on Layout." But more than that influences the situation.

Today design as a field of endeavor has become very popular and is being taken very seriously. Nearly every manufacturer now has his product "designed." It used to be that a coffee pot was made simply to be functional—just to boil some water with coffee in it, with a spout for pouring. Not today. Coffee pots, in addition to being functional, must also be "designed." That is, attention must be given to line, proportion, form, materials used, even color. In other words, coffee pots must have some aesthetic value. So it goes from perfume bottles to television sets and some types of furniture. The Museum of Modern Art in New York has staged exhibits on the design of commonplace objects.

As you would expect, schools of design have been established to teach people how to make things visually interesting and even provocative as well as functional. Sometimes designers, in their enthusiasm about design, forget function, as in the case of certain automobiles.

Here we are "designing" the basic elements of a small magazine. Of course you think first of your readers. Sex? Age? Economic and educational levels? Then you bring in the purpose of your book, and the question: how may our magazine accomplish its purpose? And the answer might be—by certain types of content. One question that comes quickly to mind is: will they need to read a considerable amount of text, or will the visual part of the book weigh heavily in accomplishing your purpose? What size page will our readers be most comfortable with? Since you are not likely to be using ads, you are not required to take that into account.

The weight of a book is influential in reader appeal. If there are few pages, perhaps 16, an 8 x 11 size is too large. Most magazines that come with Sunday newspapers are like that. It goes limp in your hand and is hard to hold. In that case you might consider a brochure-type size (6 x 9) or some variation after consulting your printer. If you can handle 36 pages, the standard 8 x 11 is possible. Mailing cost is also a factor if some of your readers are not in your location. Therefore keep the book light in weight, sometimes by the smart selection of paper stock. Again your printer can advise you.

At last we come to what your magazine should look like. And your designer, and you too if you do not have a design consultant, will likely go in for colorful (color becomes more and more important these days), attention-getting images.

If you select one of the smaller formats, 6 x 9 or 6 x 8, the magazine may be bound (usually stapled) so that the book opens horizontally instead of vertically, and the layouts will reflect the advantage of the long horizontal space of a two-page spread. *The Literary Guild Magazine* has done just that within the last year. The opportunities for striking layouts and dramatic uses of color are much enhanced. However, this plan assumes that the reader is not expected to read a lot of text. On the other hand, he would be likely to look forward to the next issue more eagerly. Such a publication would probably have a self-cover but the cover design could be just as arresting as the content.

The cover design is, in any case, an important component. The designer should dream up a logotype (the title as it appears on the cover) that is eye-catching and offers the possibility of fitting in with many types of cover design. The size is unimportant because a small one is just as appealing as a large one if the design is well done. It is a good idea to examine the various covers used today. You will have to decide whether to have the same design each time (usually without pictures) and use tag lines to lure the reader inside. If so, this plan is appropriate for more or less "serious" magazines, those read mainly by academic types. The 8 x 11 format, on the other hand, offers a chance to use a striking picture, usually tied in with some interesting feature of the content. The photo may be color or black and white. Artwork, too, is often used today. A good artist will produce in color a super eye-catcher just short of being zany, unless he has had instructions one way or the other. This would be true if the readership is expected to include teen-agers or young adults. For instance, a magazine called *Wheels* (admittedly a cliché—you can do better) addressed to members of a loose organization of people interested in biking should have something a little avant-garde about it.

The cover should not be static and it should point to, if not tell, a story that appears in that issue of the book. The only permanent feature of a cover is the logotype and it should not be changed. It furnishes necessary stability for even the wildest, most unpredictable cover. The page size should be another stable element. It used to be thought that the typography should be a part of the basic design and should be relatively stable — the body type, captions, blurbs, and the like. But designers today feel that an unnecessary limitation. As long as the typography inside and out does not clash and is in what the readers think is good taste, those old limitations can be abandoned. (Again the readers, you see.) The cover as well as the typography of a book for a woman's club would be different from one for back packers. The latter readers will not give taste even a first look, but the ladies will. Even so, a good designer will be able to sense the difference, and the latter job will be in just as good taste as the former, whether or not the reader is conscious of it. In any case, each will be "designed" in the sense we have been using that term.

As was said earlier, a freer, more impactful, and more provocative approach to design is in the practice today. Most readers appreciate it although there are some old hounds who wish the *National Geographic* had not started to put color photos on its covers.

Frequency of publication is an important matter of executive decision. Ask questions such as:

We have a mimeo job newsletter for local readers. Is there enough to say to them to justify a weekly, bi-weekly, monthly?

We have a house organ for a large but local industrial plant. Will our readers think a weekly is too much? Would a popular monthly in a small format be appealing?

We have a magazine of 96 pages that goes to a large organization of professionals. Should it be issued monthly, every two months, as a quarterly?

We have a hobby magazine. Is there enough content for a monthly? Anything less seems insignificant. Can we be more inventive in procuring copy? Should we try for a big impact, or would a 7 x 10 inch format mailed every two weeks make more sense?

Inasmuch as any printing is expensive these days, a reasonable financial economy in making these decisions is surely called for. Any one of these possibilities can be both attractive and effective.

❖ SELECTION OF A PRINTER

While this responsible decision is made by the executive(s) of the magazine it is related to basic design and so included in the decisions and consultations described in this chapter. Even if you have a four-page fold or 65 pages, there is certain information the printer must have to decide whether or not he can do the job and for what price. It is unlikely that everything will work out smoothly, so you may have to make some concessions. You need information from him, too.

MANUFACTURE. You will recall the several kinds of printing processes described in Chapter 6. Go over them in editorial consultation before you visit establishments to evaluate their work. You will recall the small and inexpensive offset process, which may seem good to you on a book with 8–16 pages in a small dimension. Also a mini-press process would be appropriate for this size. Read again the chapter on printing to see the difference between them. If your magazine is larger than 36 pages or more you will likely want to decide between letterpress or offset. In general, offset is cheaper if a lot of four-color work is what you want. But that is not always true, so you should visit the shops and talk to a person in authority. You might also ask to see the presses at work.

Any printer will need the following information from you in order to establish his cost; the same is true whether you are considering offset printing or mini-press.

1. Trim size of the magazine, that is, the outside dimensions of a single leaf.

2. Number of pages per issue.

3. Number of issues per year.

4. Number of copies of each issue to be printed.

5. Dimensions of the type page in picas.

6. The approximate number and character of the illustrations, whether line cuts or halftones or both. Also indicate whether the printer will be expected to have the engravings made or whether you will supply them, if letterpress is being considered. Unless someone in the editorial office is experienced in this field, it is probably better to make the printer responsible for the engravings.

7. Number of colors of ink for text and cover.

8. Type faces wanted, with designation of sizes for the various kinds of matter. It may be that you are not familiar enough with type faces to furnish this information. In that case, ask the printer's advice, showing him the kind of copy to be used in the magazine and explaining its purpose and slant.

9. Paper: size, weight, and kind of paper for text and

cover. Again, you may need the printer's advice before you can be definite on these points. He is prepared to tell you the advantages and disadvantages of various stocks for your job.

10. Binding, that is, whether self-covered or extra-covered, and the cover design or treatment; the process by which the pages are to be held together, that is, saddle-stitched or wired, side-wired, or sewed. Most small magazines, because of the low number of pages, can be saddle-wired. This means that wire staples are punched through the pages in the middle of the book saddlewise. In a side-wired binding, the staples are punched at the side of the pages from the top through to the bottom of the stack of signatures. If a magazine is side-wired the inside margin should be ½ inch at least. This binding gives the magazine a "bookish" feel and is appropriate for such publications as a journal of opinion or a publication in a professional field, especially one with as many as 32 to 64 pages. Sewing is more secure but more expensive and is required only by magazines with many pages. The self-covered publication is almost always saddle-wired. When it has as few as eight pages, it may even be pasted.

11. Proof: Again, in the case of letterpress, number and kind wanted, whether galleys, pages, revised pages (a second proof after alterations have been made on first page proofs), press proof (pulled after all corrections have been made and the pages are assembled in forms ready for printing). In most cases, first and second, or revised, page proofs will suffice.

12. Delivery or distribution: where the finished copies are to be delivered; or, if the printer is to mail them, whether labels, wrappers, or envelopes are to be used, and who supplies them.

On the basis of all of the above information, the printer will supply specimen pages as well as an estimate of cost. From these pages you can check your own judgments on basic design and also the quality of the printer's work. Observe especially if the inking on an offset press is adequate. You do not want an overall gray appearance. Also check the camera-ready work. Is the typing even and smooth, not wasteful of space, and accurate? Estimates and specimen pages from two or more printers will not only show differences in price but also make it possible to compare workmanship. The general appearance of the pages will show whether a printer takes pride in his work or whether this is merely another job.

THE CONTRACT. After the printer has been chosen, it may be necessary to have a formal contract. If you have a detailed estimate of cost covering all the items listed here and have worked out a schedule which you and the printer agree on, your written letter of acceptance may be sufficient. But the printer will probably wish to buy paper for your magazine in large quantities so as to get the best price. In this case he will want a year's contract. If he is to supply the photoengravings and is able to get from a subcontractor a quantity discount, he may wish a guarantee in writing. Perhaps there are unusual arrangements regarding payments that would require a formal contract. If you are operating on a tight annual budget, you may wish a year's contract for a quoted price. Most printers' bids, however, include a clause to the effect that if the cost of labor and materials increases, prices will be increased. Once an issue is started, a reliable printer will complete the job at the quoted price unless the customer is guilty of unnecessary delays.

Whether the contract is formal or informal, certain points should be covered in writing.

1. Price. At the time the estimate is requested it is well to ask that it be broken down into charges for composition (if letterpress), amount of camera-ready work (if offset), printing, and binding. The printing and binding costs should be quoted for the edition specified, with the cost of additional hundreds or thousands in units of 4, 8, or 16 pages. Wrapping and mailing costs should be given in dollars per hundred or thousand. These breakdowns are important. With them, bills may be checked accurately and arguments regarding charges may be avoided. It also makes it easier to compare prices of different printers.

2. Schedule, in terms of working days required for the delivery of proofs and bound copies.

3. Understanding as to who is to supply what in the way of materials, engravings, mailers.

4. Mailing procedures and charges, including cutting of address stencils and keeping these up to date.

After the contract is made and the specimen pages have been approved—all in advance—the manufacturing process is ready to start on the "copy to printer" scheduled date.

CHAPTER NINE

THE EDITOR AND
HIS READERS

The editor of the small magazine that we have been considering in this book sustains an unusual relationship with his readers. The commercial magazine is edited on a take-it-or-leave-it basis with every effort to persuade the reader to take it. But there the matter ends. The readers of a commercial publication can properly be thought of as "they" in the editorial office, for they have no proprietary interest in the book. In the editorial office of the publication of an organization or institution—club, league, business, industry, professional association, public agency—the situation is quite different. In a real sense, the readers and the editor are "we." Whatever the sponsoring body, its magazine is a part of its program and the constituents, therefore, may logically feel that the magazine belongs to them. They usually receive the publication by virtue of membership, and they may take the same interest in it that they do in other aspects of their organization.

From the standpoint of the editor, this at least incipient feeling of proprietorship on the part of the readers is almost pure gain. If he had to work against reader indifference and detachment, the editor would have a much harder time selling the message of the parent body. Should the readers have a detached attitude, one of his first responsibilities would be to try to win them to active participation. One of the editor's major responsibilities is to cultivate a we-are-all-in-this-together psychology, without which the cutting edge of the periodical is blunted.

This relationship is easy to see and assess in the case of the journal of an organization with members; it is less obvious, but equally important, in the case of the house publication distributed to employees. All too often the house magazine appears to its readers as the voice of one department or even the top administration talking to the readers about things in which they should be interested. Employees have strong defenses against being "told" by employers, even concerning matters in their own interest. For the magazine to speak realistically *with* and not *to* the readers, the editor should foster on their part a feeling of identification with the participation in the book. This is the "we" and not the "they" frame of reference.

This editorial relationship shows up the one disadvantage of delegating responsibility for house publications to an outside concern, such as an advertising agency. What the book gains in the professional touch, it loses in personal appeal and reader identification. (An exception would be the house publication circulated to customers.) It would be better to tie the editorial management of an employee magazine closely to the employees themselves. Appropriate and effective ways of building up a strong relationship between the editor and his readers are described below.

❧ PERSONAL CONTACT

It has been pointed out in several connections in the foregoing chapters that the editor must know his readers. It is also important that the readers know the editor, not only vicariously through the pages of the magazine, but directly through personal contacts. Through such contacts the book comes to life, it becomes more than something that is produced in a remote and impersonal office. Both reader identification and reader participation depend to a large extent on communication between editor and readers.

One of the duties of the editor, therefore, is to get about among his readers so as to facilitate this communication. If the book is locally circulated to a closely knit group, this is no problem—in fact, it may happen in the normal round of affairs. But if the book has a decentralized readership, for example, if it comprises members of local units of a national body or scattered branches of a business or industry, the editor's personal contacts must be planned and organized. In the budget of the editorial office, an item should be provided for visits by the editor to key places where he may become acquainted with various sections of his constituency. Perhaps he will visit one of the different branches each year to meet and talk with people, collecting material for stories and absorbing reader reaction. He can also use this occasion for cultivating his local reporters. At a national or regional meeting of the parent body where large numbers of his readers will gather, the editor should be present and probably organize some institutional promotion for the magazine.

The purpose of this promotion is not to get subscriptions, which are usually included in membership dues or handled by local units of the organization, but to call attention to the magazine, to stimulate interest, and to gain favorable response. A brochure printed in the format of the magazine and containing the program of the meeting as well as items of current interest may be a good promotional scheme. The magazine might sponsor at a large convention a lounge for the delegates where posters and other display pieces may furnish pertinent information about the magazine. Again, at a large convention lasting several days, the magazine might issue a daily bulletin of features which would be useful or of interest to the delegates, including some announcements designed to make readers look forward to future issues of the magazine. The editor should circulate freely at such gatherings to collect the impressions of his readers and, conversely, to allow his readers to gain inside impressions of the magazine. If local reporters are present, he should plan to get them together for a combined business and social session where they would have full opportunity to interpret reader point of view and to consult with the editor. Through these devices and the personal contacts they provide, the editor gets ideas for stories, and he can keep a check on basic editorial policy after several such occasions. And for the reader, they serve the purpose of personalizing the publication.

❋ CORRESPONDENCE

At several points, heretofore, letters to the editor to be published in the magazine have been discussed. Letters not destined for publication are also important. They are a form of communication between the editor and his readers. They may be solicited through the pages of the magazine on points of policy or on proposed programs or on an item for which reader reaction would be mutually beneficial, thus enabling the reader to participate in the magazine's activities and the editor to have firsthand response.

If the readers know that the editorial office is open for comments, much of the correspondence will be unsolicited. Response of this sort is often the best kind. Every unsolicited letter should be answered, especially if it contains a negative reaction. When people feel a sense of proprietorship, they are likely to be critical, and sometimes the criticism will be negative. The editor should understand that this attitude is healthy and desirable and that he can learn as much from reactions against as from those in favor of some aspect or feature of the magazine. Criticism that is constructive and made in good faith should be seriously received. It may or may not alter policy, because the editor and his executive must weigh each comment as to the number of readers any one correspondent can be considered to speak for. And the readers who never write to the editor must be taken into account in evaluations.

A word of warning should be included here. The magazine must never be allowed to become the battleground for an intramural struggle in the organization. The purpose of the magazine is to bring members together, not to divide them into factions, even by serving as referee. Nevertheless, the magazine may very well not be able to ignore the existence of such a struggle. This is, however, official business of the parent body, and it should be treated as such. The matter can be recognized in the pages of the magazine through words from the organization's official spokesmen, acting as statesmen, not as protagonists. This is a policy the editor and his executive should insist upon. Otherwise, the magazine may not survive the struggle.

❖ THE EDITORIAL BOARD

One of the best mediums for achieving reader participation in a magazine with a widespread constituency is the editorial board composed of reader representatives. The functions of such a board are to survey and evaluate past issues of the magazine, to advise with the editor on future plans, to suggest content and policy, and, in general, to speak for the readership. The members of the board may be either appointed by the editor in consultation with the executive and officers of the parent body or elected by the membership. Usually the appointed board is more useful to the editor because its members may be selected according to proper qualifications. The elected board, however, may be a better instrument for gaining reader identification, as the members may feel that through it they are more truly represented. In either case, the members should be drawn from the rank and file of the constituency, the number depending upon the size of the parent body and the logistics of arranging meetings.

The status of an editorial board is advisory, never executive. It should have no legal or constitutional responsibility for the magazine. This authority and responsibility must rest with elected officers and executives of the organization. That is not to say that the editorial board may not be very influential. Because it speaks for the readers at large, its voice should carry much weight with those responsible for planning the magazine. In the case of an employee publication, administrative relationships are not impaired by an editorial advisory board; ultimate responsibility is lodged in the appropriate department. But board members can give excellent counsel in shaping editorial policy and practice so as to keep the magazine in line with the real interests and concerns of its readers. Thus, the publication may be clearly identified with its readers and not with the top administration of the organization. Top administrators should take the view that this is not abdicating their responsibility, but executing it in an effective fashion. The functions of this board should be clearly distinguished from the planning conference described in Chapter 1.

Probably once a year is as often as an editorial board should meet. The editor, his executive, and perhaps the appropriate elected officers of the organization should plan the meeting carefully, so that it will be really fruitful. A letter to board members may solicit items for the agenda and so involve the board in planning its own meeting. Notice of the board meeting may be printed in the magazine with a request for suggestions from readers. Then the meeting should be reported with as much detail as practical.

An editorial board may undertake surveys to obtain data that would be useful to the magazine. For example, suppose program suggestions for local units of a national organization have been printed in its journal over a period of time. The editorial board might well conduct a survey to find out more precisely than their personal impressions would indicate whether the material has been effective.

Surveys to discover relative popularity of regular items of content are also a possibility. An analysis of the readership to determine what the profile of the "normal" reader looks like is another type of survey. Reaction of the members of the organization to a nation-wide program emphasis lends itself to study through the magazine.

As useful as an editorial board is in enlisting participation of the readers, it has definite limitations. It can never do the editor's job for him, and should not be expected to do it. This board represents the readers' point of view, which is naturally different from the editor's. Therein lies its value to the editor. Reduced to simple terms, the board can advise *what* to do but has little judgment as to *how*. The latter is the responsibility of the editorial office. For example, the board may suggest "something on hobbies" but not have any idea how specific features appropriate to the book can be organized and developed. Or the members may say the publication looks a little dull and want the pages livened up, but they are probably unable to suggest ways of doing it. The follow-through involving technique and method requires the editor's journalistic skill. Also, it should be understood by all that the board is not a planning group. When plans are made, account is taken of reactions and suggestions from board members. But the editorial board does not edit the magazine; it advises the editor from the standpoint of the readers.

Through these formal means—personal contacts, correspondence, an editorial board—in addition to many informal ones, the editor keeps open channels of communication with his readers and maintains a relationship of mutuality. He encourages their sense of identification with the magazine, so that the message and the program of the sponsoring organization are seen as their own, and not as something outside their immediate orbit or alien to their interests.

There are editors who seldom take a look at the magazine once it is in print. They plead the rush of oncoming issues, disappointment with plans that went awry, frustration on encountering the inevitable mistakes, or just plain boredom with having seen the stuff all too frequently. It is an understandable attitude. But every so often every editor should retreat to whatever sanctum is available and closet himself with a year's issues. Then, as he turns the pages, he should ask himself these questions: What do I find here that is relevant to the real interests of my readers? What questions of theirs are being answered, or at least dealt with? Are these pages accessible to my readers so that they quickly get the point of each feature? Of what significance are the various features to my readers?

The answers to these questions will indicate where the editor should concentrate his effort in the months ahead.

❖
THE EDITOR'S BOOKSHELF

Every practicing editor should have within reach of his mind as well as his hand a few of the most valuable resources to increase his skill as a practitioner.

A reliable dictionary comes first because it is usually most consulted and contains, in addition to definitions, spelling, derivations of words, pronunciations, alphabets, proof readers' marks, and the like. What is a reliable dictionary? One that you can use with confidence.

For many years *Webster's New Collegiate Dictionary* (G. and C. Merriam Co., second edition) was recommended to ease quickly the editor's path. Some editorial offices invest in the Merriam-Webster unabridged dictionary, *Webster's New International Dictionary*.

In 1967, however, Merriam brought out what it referred to as its "Third Edition," causing an uproar among teachers, scholars, librarians, editors, and other people who commonly use dictionaries. What caused the storm was the fact that the company had changed its policy drastically. Instead of being a reliable and accepted *standard*, derived from historical and some contemporary usages by persons of literary repute, it became, as they said, a "reporting" of the way people use the language today—all people, not just those whose writing is considered correct because of the literary reputation of the user.

"Standards," that is, the usage that is accepted as correct, had suddenly dissolved, to the consternation mostly of teachers and scholars. The word "ain't" is entered as allowable spelling and usage. The Webster editors say "why not?" Who has the authority to decide what is "correct" in English speech? The question is a poser. It seems clear that the decision was made out of the spirit of "doing your own thing," getting away from the implicitly elitist view of "W-2" that "This is right, and no questions, please." But, carried to its logical conclusion, chaos would prevail in English speech and writing without any agreed-upon standards and forms. Communication would be almost impossible.

Of course, "W-3" does not intend anything like that. It seems rather that the purpose was to open up the language, to submit it to less rigidity and at least to appear more democratic in quoting, for example, Mae West as an example of correct English as well as Virginia Woolf.

The controversy has died down somewhat, the chief fallout having been the production of several very good dictionaries that compete with the "W-3" collegiate editions ("W-2" is out of print). Highly recommended as a desk dictionary, although somewhat large in format even for that, is the *American Heritage Dictionary of the English Language* (Houghton Mifflin). Its good points include particular attention to derivations of words, its inclusion of really contemporary words, its pictures in the margins, and its fresh and lively style.

Webster's Dictionary of Synonyms (G. & C. Merriam Company) is a useful source for determining precise meanings and connotations of words, for distinguishing among words with similar or related meanings, and for discovering substitutes for overused words. The subtitle of this volume explains its content: A *Dictionary of Discriminated Synonyms with Antonyms and Analogous and Contrasted Words.* For the person who has a real enthusiasm for words, this book is a treasure house.

But an editor needs more than a dictionary, so we turn now to books about style. They deal with commonplace issues such as the "that" versus "which" problem and the "sequence of tenses," as well as with the less commonplace issues of the language.

It has already been stated that every editor needs an official stylebook which will be standard for everyone in the office because it can settle matters that people disagree on, each being correct. A simple example: "red, white and blue" *or* "red, white, and blue." Many editorial offices use as their official guide A *Manual of Style* (The University of Chicago Press). It covers the major topics of concern to the copyreader, the proofreader, and others involved in preparing and handling proof.

In addition, among the first great books of this kind in our day is A *Dictionary of Modern English Usage* by H. W. Fowler, an English scholar. For years "Fowler" has been the court of last appeal. But even he can slip into history; also, the English and American languages differ in meanings and references, so it is good to have A *Dictionary of Modern American-English Usage,* by Margaret Nicholson, which updates Fowler. This is really not a stylebook but a comprehensive guide to using the English language accurately, clearly, and precisely.

Then we have, published in 1966, *Modern American Usage, A Guide,* by Wilson Follett. He died before completing his work and the finished volume says "Edited and Completed by Jacques Barzun in collaboration with Carlos Baker, Frederick W. Dupee, Dudley Fitts, James D. Hart, Phyllis McGinley, and Lionel Trilling."

Published in 1973, a book entitled A *Dictionary of Usage and Style, The Reference Guide for Professional Writers, Editors, Reporters, Teachers, and Students,* by Roy H. Copperud, takes a somewhat different approach and so increases its usefulness. It is published by Hill and Wang.

A popular volume on style should be added because, in addition to being a professional aid, it is a pleasure to read: *The Elements of Style,* by William Strunk and E. B. White. Mr. White not long ago retired from the staff of *The New Yorker* magazine and still occasionally contributes a clever and pungent piece. Mr. Strunk was one of Mr. White's favorite teachers at Cornell University. In 1959 Macmillan decided to bring out a new edition, as the title of the subhead says, "With Revisions, an Introduction, and a New Chapter on Writing" by E. B. White. Be sure not to miss this one.

We have alluded several times to the legal aspects of the

editor's job. One of the most frequent of these is the matter of copyright. The definitive treatment is *A Manual on Copyright Practice*, by Margaret Nicholson (Oxford University Press).

The application of the principles of communication to the editorial task was interpreted briefly in an earlier chapter. Some resources in this field may profitably be included in the editor's expanded library. Two titles on this subject are recommended: *Anatomy of Writing*, by Peter Swiggart (Prentice-Hall, Inc.), and *The Technique of Clear Writing*, by Robert C. Gunning (McGraw-Hill Book Company). Both of these books have to do with the practice of communicative writing and not so much with the theory of communication as such. Closely related to communication is the subject of semantics. Here it is easy to get far afield from the typical concerns of the editor of the small magazine. But at least an elementary approach to semantics (the science of meanings) helps the editor in predicting and assessing general reader response to his pages. *The Reader over Your Shoulder*, by Graves and Hodge (The Macmillan Company), serves as an excellent introduction to this field and assists the editor in that indispensable editorial practice, keeping his mind on his readers. A small operation should also have access to a good encyclopedia, and we recommend without reservation, and without solicitation of any kind, *The New Columbia Encyclopedia*, in one volume (Columbia University Press).

A secondary function of all these books is to keep the editor related to the magazine world and to publishing in general. Although his profession may be in another area and his main interests may tend to lead him in another direction, the editor of the small magazine should strive to be at least somewhat knowledgeable in the publication business. Only by so doing can he keep his periodical lively and directly related to his readers.

INDEX